Step Into Your Legacy

The Journey to Become the Man
You've Been Called to Be

A Memoir

A. Shepherd Jordan

ISBN: 978-1-998188-00-0 (paperback)
ISBN: 978-1-998188-01-7 (hardcover)
ISBN: 978-1-998188-02-4 (ebook)

Available in paperback, hardcover, e-book, and audiobook

Published by Reachout Publishing
PO Box 159, Clyde, Alberta T0G 0P0

www.reachloveconnect.com

Dedication

To my brother Jimmy,

The 4th of his name
My first and longest tenured role model and mentor
It hasn't always been easy, but you were always my
brother.

Contents

Prologue — V

• Here's the problem

Introduction — XIII

• Laying down the challenge

1. In the Beginning — 1

• My story and how it relates to the rest of the book

2. Mike Keville — 13

• Heroes come in all shapes and sizes
• It only takes a second to make an impact that lasts a lifetime

3. Dave Boettger — 41

• You don't have to be the most talented to be the most valuable
• Adversity is the foundation for success

4. Jett Colonna — 69

• Knowing when and how to be a warrior
• Knowing when and how to be kindhearted

5. Dave Trickler — 99

• The importance of preparation, fundamentals, and execution
• How to motivate people and a team

6. Royce Jones — 131

- How you play the game, whether its football or life, is more important than whether you win or lose
- Rising above your circumstances

7. James M. Jordan, III — 161

- When things don't turn out the way you planned them
- Leaving a legacy

Epilogue — 193

- Coming full circle
- Your marching orders

Endorsements — 203

Acknowledgements — 207

Prologue

"The Lord God took the man and put him in the Garden of Eden to work it and take care of it."

Genesis 2:15

"Mentors, by definition, have already walked where you are about to step, and they've had time to process the lessons along the way."

From *Hinge Moments* by D. Michael Lindsay

I wonder, have you noticed?

If you're a male, especially an adult male, I'll bet you have noticed and not just because I'm asking the question now. Here's what I'm driving at: have you noticed that it's becoming more and more difficult to know what it means to be a man, a good man in the world today? Specifically, what role(s) would you say today's male serves in our society and exactly how does one learn those roles?

These are questions I honestly never considered when I was a younger man and, depending on your age, maybe you haven't either. But now that I've reached the "back nine of life," I can look back and observe how the role of men in our society has slowly, over the last several decades, become distorted to the point where there is now near zero clarity or consensus.

I got my first glimpse of this dilemma back in 1997 when I began a career in secondary education. The changes for men at that time were subtle, but I could sense that expectations and values for young males had become slightly different than when I had been a student in the early 70's. Qualities that I had learned and understood to define a good man, things like high moral character and integrity, accountability, humility, and a strong work ethic, no longer seemed to be the expectations for the youth I encountered.

By the time I left education in 2017, that change had

become, in my view, somewhat pandemic in nature; everyone seemed to be confused or unsure about the righteous role for a male in the modern world. If you were to ask 10 young men what they believed it means to be a good man these days, I bet you would likely get that many different answers.

And so, I wonder, has it always been this difficult to know what it means to be a man?

No, I don't think it has.

Here's something to consider: in the book of Genesis, the very first book of the Bible, chapter 2 verse 15, we see that God put Adam, the first man, into the Garden of Eden to "work it and take care of it," no small task. So, at least from a biblical perspective, our purpose and meaning as men seems clear. We are meant to work and take care of things that are important. Even if you are not of the Christian world view, I have to ask, is it a stretch to think it might just be that simple?

The problem is our modern culture has made it much more complicated and confusing than it should or needs to be. I came to this conclusion after spending several years thinking back and reflecting on my own journey to manhood back in the '60s and '70s, trying to piece together how I came to understand the proper role of men in our world. What exactly, I wondered, is the best course toward living a meaningful, responsible life as a man? It didn't seem to be so complicated when I was younger. So, what's changed?

One of the byproducts of my time of reflection is a greater understanding of how we, as a society, have reached the point where many men are confused about their role and purpose in life, who they want to be or who they should be. Our goals, our definition of manhood, have been radically altered by television, films and the internet.

To say the least, a lot has changed in our often tech-no-savvy, twenty-four-hour news cycle world but the changing world is not the primary focus of this book. My focus is on how a man can maintain a stable and honest sense of self amidst dizzying change. Sure, I could bore you with statistics and stories about the profoundly negative impacts that fatherless homes and dead-beat dads have on young boys, but there have been countless books already written along those exact subject lines. You don't need me to throw more data at you!

I've decided to take a different approach in offering a solution to this problem. First, I start with the logical presumption that a home with a father who is present and not abusive in any way is generally a good thing. Nevertheless, as I drilled down deeper into my past I realized even that stability is not always enough to create honorable young men. By dusting off my long-ago dormant memories, I came to agree with the familiar, old cliché that it takes a village to raise a child. It certainly did for me. I believe it still does. The simple fact is that role models and mentors do matter and they are of critical importance, especially when it comes to setting the right foundation for boys and young men to help them become the men God intends them to be. Sadly, my observation has been that there are fewer and fewer men worthy of the title these days. It would seem that we no longer know what it takes to be a good role model and mentor or what that even looks like.

This book is meant to bring clarity to that question by offering you six stories that dramatize what I believe good role models and mentors look like. I was blessed to have a dad who was always present and an excellent role model for me. But, as the memories of my youth came into focus, I was reminded there were also other men, five otherwise ordinary but good men, who crossed my path when I was between the ages of 9 and 19. These five men kept coming back to my mind when I was wrestling with trying to understand what it takes to be a good role model and mentor. Their stories and how they profoundly impacted me are intended to show you all you'll ever need to know about what a good role model and mentor looks like. Their example will serve as a "roadmap" for you as you assume the inevitable responsibility yourself one day.

Some final words. You may already have recognized that the underlying foundation for the content of this book is the Christian faith, but please don't let that deter you if you are not of that world view. Whatever your beliefs, in my heart I believe that the principles and values held in common by my six good men should apply to men of all religions, all cultures, all races and in all countries. Nevertheless, my life experience has proven to me many times over that the best model of what God intends us to be as men, comes from the pages of His inspired word, which is the Bible.

Also remember that this book is a memoir and as such, depends on my own recollection of the people and events I write about. It's entirely likely that my six men didn't have the kind of impact on others as they did me because, as with any great teacher, the impact is always personal and not necessarily universal.

What's most important are the lessons that each of us can learn. What's crucial is how each of us finds a way of passing along the wisdom and grace that have been given to us, one individual to the next, the circle ever widening, the village expanding.

I hope you enjoy the journey and adventures I share with you. My intention is that the stories will compel you to recall your own, perhaps forgotten story. I hope it pushes you to reach back into your own past and re-discover those men who acted as role models and mentors in your life, the men who helped define the man you are today.

Introduction

"Stand at the crossroads and look; ask for the ancient
paths, ask where the good way is, and walk in it,
and you will find rest for your souls."

Jeremiah 6:16

"This is every man's deepest fear: to be exposed, to be
found out, to be discovered as an imposter, and
not really a man."

From *Wild at Heart* by John Eldredge

Doesn't it seem as though everyone is clamoring for attention these days? Perhaps you've recognized that lately the need to define one's identity in this world has become a major and singular focus for many. It's not especially difficult to understand why this is; it's part of our nature as humans to want to feel as though we are validated and loved, that we're important.

Without a doubt, social media and technology have played a significant part in the rapid development of the ever-growing need to self-promote. The challenge though, especially in the current cultural climate, is knowing how to manage this need in a way that's honorable, responsible, and not at the expense of others. As a society, we're not doing a very good job with this right now.

I once worked for a person who would callously declare at meetings of those that worked under him, "if you do your job you get to keep it." Statements like this are what I refer to as negative reinforcement, an oxymoron, surely. On the surface, its intent is to provide motivation (or is it?), but it comes in a negative way. Fortunately for me, I was at a point in life where I knew and understood that this style of leadership is, by its nature, toxic and designed to tear down rather than build up. Not at all a good example to be modeling and I believe we're seeing much more of that kind of attitude prevailing in the world these days. I wish I was wrong about that.

What concerns me the most, though, is how much of our identity is shaped and formed by the role models and mentors we encounter, especially early in our lives. For the sake of clarity, I define a role model as someone who offers a standard to achieve while mentors show you and help you to achieve that standard. The two, in my view, go hand in hand and it's rare for great role models not to also be great mentors. In this book you will notice I use both terms interchangeably.

So, I'd like to take you back to your pre-adolescent and adolescent days. You might remember that was the time in your life when you first began your own search for an identity, your identity. It likely wasn't a conscious search; it wasn't for me, but I think for most at that age, the tendency is to look for things that will say to the world, this is who I am. Maybe it's a talent for music or a passion for sports. Perhaps it could be a love for all things technological or it could define itself as an entrepreneurial spirit. Regardless of what that thing may be, your identity will grow as you invest time in developing it. And as that investment grows, so will your competence and sense of self.

It's important to note here however, that what drives males and females in terms of their sense of self and competence is not necessarily the same. In their best-selling books, "For Men Only" and "For Women Only," husband and wife authors Shaunti and Jeff Feldhahn get right to the heart of the matter. After conducting thousands of surveys of both men and women it comes down to this: the one thing women say they desire the most is to feel secure and loved. However, they found that for men, even more important than feeling loved was feeling respected.

It's a very important distinction.

From my earliest days and until I left for college, it was

sports, football and lacrosse specifically, that I chose to define me. I saw myself, my identity, as an athlete, and it was through sports that I would seek to earn the respect all males hope to attain.

So, why did I choose sports?

The simple answer is that I loved sports, but I was also following in the footsteps of my earliest and most influential role models: my father and two older brothers. All three had been excellent athletes in their day, especially in football. It seemed only natural to me to follow their lead.

In my constant pursuit to establish an identity through sports I came in to contact with quite a few role models. As you will see, a handful were instrumental in my positive development and identity as a man. But I learned early in high school that sometimes life is going to challenge you in ways you never expected.

When I was a junior in high school, I had one coach who, like my example above, preferred to use negative reinforcement to try and motivate players. In retrospect, I'm sure I was just being a little sensitive but at the time it seemed to me I was the one player he used that tactic on the most. The negative reinforcement seemed relentless. Unfortunately, it had the exact opposite of his intended outcomes for me. Instead of motivating me, it led me to question and even doubt my worth. This, in turn, put a major dent in my identity and led me to question my sense of self as an athlete and as a male. It wasn't long before I desperately wanted to do something I'd never done: quit.

But my dad wouldn't let me. His message to me was one we rarely hear these days: "Shep, I understand your reasons for wanting to quit. But you made a commitment for this season, and you need to see it through no matter what. If you don't want to play next year that's fine, but you started this season, you need to finish it."

I finished the season. It was the worst three months of my teenage life. I came to realize later though that dad was right and I'm grateful he convinced me stick it out. In a perfect example of role modelling and mentoring, dad taught me a valuable life lesson that he himself had learned many years prior as a promising high school football player: no matter how difficult the circumstances, quitting is never an option. When you make a commitment, you see it through to the end.

It's been almost 50 years since that time and I have long ago come to terms with that one negative experience. But I'll never lose the awareness of the profound impact losing of my sense of self had on me as I grew into adulthood. I think intuitively I knew it even back then, but it took many years for me to fully grasp the significance and impact role models can have on the life of a young person. I came to fully understand and embrace their importance as I grew older, had sons of my own, and became a teacher/coach myself. It forced me to draw from and evaluate my own experiences.

You may have had good and/or bad role models in your life but what matters most are the lessons you can learn from those experiences. At some point in your life, you will likely be thrust into the position of role model and mentor. In that role, you'll have absolute power to make either a positive or negative impact on someone. How you choose to use that power will have profound and long-lasting consequences.

In this book I'm going to share the stories of six ordinary men who made an indelible, positive impact on me during my adolescence. Though most were coaches or teachers, one was a student in college. Not the least of these was my dad. Each of these men taught me by words and actions, what it means to be a "good man" and how to live a life with integrity, accountability, confidence, and humility. Each had his own set of personal flaws and life challenges. Yet, despite their challenges, each was the kind of role model every young guy would hope to have. These men set a standard that I try to emulate every day of my life.

Unfortunately, the statistics reveal that these days not every boy is blessed, like I was, to have the kind of positive role models they need in their lives. My hope is that this book can be not only a narrative of hope but a training manual for role models and mentors, as well.

Whether you realize it or not, like it or not…someday some young guy or group of guys is going to look up to you as a role model. Most likely those young men will include your sons and other family members. But they also might be co-workers, neighbors, or those you teach or coach. They'll be looking up to you to learn how to live life as a man … a good man. Will you be worthy of the trust they put in you? Will you, through your actions and words be able to guide them in a positive way as they seek answers to the questions, they, like all males, desperately need to hear: Do I measure up? Do I have what it takes?

It's an enormous responsibility being a role model and mentor. The good news is you'll see through the stories of my six 'heroes' that you don't have to be a Superman. As Pulitzer Prize-winning author Robert Coles states in his book, *The Moral Intelligence of Children*, you simply need to remember this, "the child is a witness; the child is an ever attentive witness of grown-up morality – or lack thereof; the child looks and looks for cues as to how one ought to behave, and finds them galore as we parents and teachers go about our lives, making choices, addressing people, showing in action our rock-bottom assumptions, desires, and values, and thereby telling those young observers much more than we may realize."

The bottom line is you just have to be vigilant in consistently doing the right thing for those you mentor. My intention is that these stories will inspire you to reflect on your own path to manhood and the male mentors you encountered along the way, giving you direction as you answer your own call to lead younger men down the right path in life.

There are young men desperately depending on you.

Are you ready?

1

In the Beginning

"It is easier to build strong children than to repair broken men."

Frederick Douglas

"It's a character-building experience"

Mom

I knew when mom told me we had a meeting with Mr. Cumiskey that something big was up. It was early June of 1969 and the school year had just wrapped up.

"What does he want to meet about?" I inquired anxiously.

"Well, he just wants to go over your year," she said.

Charles J. Cumiskey was the Head of the Lower School (grades 1-7) at Norfolk Academy, a 1-12 independent, college preparatory school, where I had been a student since the fall of 1966. All the students revered and feared "Mr. C." There was never any doubt about his compassion and concern for the students in his charge. Just as obvious was his philosophy on behavior: actions have consequences and no matter who you were, Mr. C would hold you accountable if you crossed the line. I'm certain he was one of the originators of the philosophy of tough love. So, this meeting, at the end of my 6th grade year, had me a little nervous.

"Am I in trouble?" I asked mom, trying to recall if I had done something stupid in the last weeks of school.

"No," she said. "We just want to talk about the year you had and what we can do about it."

It had not been a good year in a number of ways, and I was feeling it. I had struggled both academically and socially. I was exhausted. This wouldn't be the first time I'd had to meet with Mr. C and I wasn't looking forward to it. I wondered how things had gotten to this point.

My oldest brother, Jimmy, used to say to me when I was younger, "You know, everyone has a story." This revelation usually came in response to my having expressed a degree of frustration over how someone else was behaving. Since Jimmy was one of my first role models, I took him at his word even if I didn't fully understand the significance of what he meant.

As I got older though, his meaning became clear to me. Jimmy's point was that everyone's life is impacted and affected by things we may know nothing about. Everyone's life is a unique and ever-changing story which gives each person's life significance and meaning.

Once I understood that, I began to marvel at how every person's story is in large part dependent on the circumstances, influences, and influencers in their life. For instance, has there ever been a time when you've looked at two or more siblings and wondered, "they are so different, how did they grow up in the same house?" Even if you grow up in the same house, your life story may end up being totally different from that of your siblings. We all react, respond, and learn differently from the myriad of influences we encounter every day.

With that in mind, my story begins in 1956.

The only remarkable thing about my birth in November of that year is that it happened at all. My mom and dad had not intended on having any more children after the birth of my sister Catherine in 1952. They had finally gotten a daughter to round out the "team" which already included my older brothers Jimmy and Fred. But my arrival four years after my sister was proof positive that things don't always turn out the way you plan them. At the time, dad was 35 years old and my mom, 34. Back then that was considered late to be having children and even a tad scandalous by the standards of the day. The story goes that when mom told dad the news of her pregnancy, he suggested that the doctor was a "quack" and that it must be a tumor or something. He was kidding of course, but I think mom's unexpected pregnancy may have been a little embarrassing for them. For as long as I can remember they claimed to have used every precaution to ensure there wouldn't be any "mistakes." Nevertheless, mom always said I was, "the best mistake they ever made." I never doubted that I was loved.

I grew up in what was then the small resort town of Virginia Beach, Virginia. With my arrival, I became the 14th out of what would eventually be 15 in my immediate family of siblings and first cousins. Of those 15, all but my younger cousin Molly and I were born between the years of 1943 and 1952, with **11** having been born in the 3-year span of 1949-1952.

I mention all of this to point out that birth order plays an extremely important role in the early development of any child. It certainly did for me. Typically, when you're the first born, your first role models are your parents, who are naturally focused solely on you. Over time though, that parental attention becomes divided as subsequent siblings arrive. Consequently, younger siblings tend to look first to their older siblings/cousins as role models. I certainly had a lot to choose from but the challenge for me was that they were all somewhat older than me.

The nearest male in age to me was my cousin Billy, who was 3 years older and lived in the neighboring city of Norfolk. I saw him maybe a couple of times a year during the holidays. As for my brothers, Jimmy is 11 years my senior and Fred 8 years. They both went away to boarding school, so I rarely saw either of them. Even if they had been home all year, their worlds and mine were light years apart at that point in our lives. They were focused on girls, sports and Motown music while I was busy watching cartoons and wondering what it was about girls that was so interesting to them. Even so, I idolized both and naturally looked to them as role models in my earliest years.

Dad would sometimes say, "when you're little, your problems are little but when you get bigger, your problems get bigger."

As I got older, I found that to be true but when you're the youngest in your family it's almost a certainty that your problems and concerns will never be as big as your older siblings and cousins. Inevitably, your problems and the things that really matter to you, never seem to get the attention you so desperately seek. Whenever I expressed my frustration about this mom would always "reassure" me by saying, "don't worry honey, your day will come." That was never the answer I was looking for.

From kindergarten through 4th grade I attended Everett School, a small (K-8th grade), independent, neighborhood school in Virginia Beach which was run by two of my aunts. By that association alone I had a degree of significance and status amongst my peers. I was an important fish in a small sea.

That all changed in the fall of 1966 when many of us from Everett left to attend Norfolk Academy in neighboring Norfolk. In an instant, I went from being something of a "royal" character to a barely visible small fish in a vast ocean. It was an adjustment from my protected, comfortable world at Everett School. Even so, I was pumped to be going to NA if for no other reason than they had sports; I mean real teams with uniforms. My dad and both brothers had been football players and good athletes at their schools, and by God, I was going to be one just like them. Like many young boys, I had visions of glory.

I started out at Norfolk Academy by repeating the 4th grade. I had been one of the youngest in my class at Everett so repeating was not a bad idea and I remained with my peer group. The thought was it would help me with the transition to a more challenging academic and social environment. For a little over a year, that proved to be a good choice. But then, towards the end of my 5th grade year, I started having trouble keeping up. Academically, I wasn't picking up on things as quickly as my classmates and I began having trouble concentrating and getting my work done. In the highly competitive environment that is the foundation of the Norfolk Academy system of education, I gradually became seen by all as a classic underachiever. I started to believe it myself.

Numerous parent/teacher conferences ensued along with several Saturday detentions, courtesy of Mr. C, due to my sometimes impulsive (and poor) behavior choices. No one seemed to be able to put a finger on the problem. The usual response from teachers/administrators was, "Shep is very capable but he's just not doing the work "or "he seems somewhat immature for his age." Mom and dad's solution was simple: I just needed to "buckle down" and work harder. Little did we know then what was really going on.

It wasn't until 1980 that the medical world coined the term attention deficit disorder (ADD). Prior to that, beginning in 1968, the same condition was something called, "hyperkinetic reaction of childhood." Who knew I was suffering from ADD? Well, nobody, because it was not widely studied until the 1980s. The same is true for the study of developmental delays or, to put it another way, not maturing socially or cognitively at a level commensurate with your age group. Fortunately, for many of the kids challenged by these issues today, the world has a scientifically proven explanation and strategies (other than just work harder) for the behaviors I struggled with as a child.

None of that was on my mind the morning my mom and I entered the Lower School building for our meeting with Mr. Cumiskey. Relatively speaking, Charley Cumiskey was not necessarily an imposing figure. Standing about 5'10" tall, he had been a standout baseball player in his days at Lynchburg College, before starting a lifelong dedication to education. This would be my last meeting with him as he was leaving Norfolk Academy to take a Head of School position at another school. Honestly, I was a little sad because I adored Mr. C. Even though I had given him cause to hold me accountable a handful of times, he was completely fair each time, and I knew I deserved the punishment. I trusted him.

Like all good role models and mentors, Mr. C had a knack for being able to communicate with young people. He never talked down to you in a condescending way; it was more like he was talking with you, even when he was letting you have it when you screwed up.

He started the meeting by asking me, "So Shep, how do you think the year went for you?"

There was no BS-ing Mr. C, so I said, "not so good, sir."

"I agree," he replied, "why do you think that is?"

Well, there he had me so I said, "I'm not sure sir, sometimes I get behind and just can't seem to catch back up. It's really frustrating."

"I agree with you", he said, "but I want to tell you I see a lot of potential in you both academically and athletically."

Back in my day, Norfolk Academy had an extensive intramural athletic program in both the Lower and Middle Schools. Beginning in 4th grade, boys played tackle, yes, tackle football in the fall, basketball, wrestling and soccer in the winter and softball and track in the spring. Mr. Cumiskey spent a good amount of time observing in the classrooms and the athletic fields, so his observations of me were not hollow words. That positive reinforcement from Mr. C was incredibly uplifting, especially after a year of hearing nothing but comments about not measuring up.

My joy was short-lived, however.

"Your parents and I have talked about it", he said, "and we think that, even though you passed all your subjects, it would be best if you repeated 6th grade next year."

There's a popular term these days to describe this moment in my life. It's called a hinge moment or, to be specific, a singular opportunity to open or to close the doors to various pathways in life. Whichever path you chose though, as stated so eloquently by the poet Robert Frost, will likely have a significant impact on the rest of your life.

In the depths of my soul, I was relieved. I knew this one decision would take some of the academic pressure off me and I would get a fresh start. On the other hand, the stigma attached to having "failed" would add an unwanted degree of social pressure.

Mr. C did his best to paint a positive picture claiming it was "no disgrace" to be repeating. I appreciated his concern but I knew it was a done deal. As the meeting ended, I thanked him and wished him the best of luck in his new position. In a couple of weeks, I would be starting the NA summer sports camp for six weeks and I would worry about all this later.

As I look back at this time in my life, I realize I have so much to be grateful for. I was part of a loving family, I attended a great school, I had a small but solid group of friends and I lived in a cool town. Despite these blessings though, I felt lost, alone, and unsure of myself and those feelings continued to a degree through high school. Both my brothers were away at school and my sister pretty much wanted nothing to do with me. I mean, what big sisters do, right?

Dad was working 12 hours a day, 6 days a week at this point, helping to expand a family hardware and building materials business that was never his passion. Mom also worked full time as a librarian at Norfolk Academy, while simultaneously managing the household.

The simple fact is there just wasn't adequate time for me at a time when I so desperately needed help navigating and understanding this thing called life. Sadly, I think this is true for far more boys and young men these days than it was for me 50 years ago. That's why it now seems so urgently important that male role models and mentors step up and lead the way for the younger generations.

We all need guidance as we navigate the path of life. We all need role models and mentors to help with that navigation. Back at that moment in sixth grade and in the years that followed, I could have easily lost my way if it hadn't been for the unexpected guides along my path. They showed me what it means to be a man, a good man. This is more their story than it is mine, and the stage is now set for you to begin the journey with me and six otherwise ordinary men who, to me, were extraordinary.

In an important way, my story really begins in the summer

of 1966 with Mike Keville, a college student and lifeguard, and comes full circle, concluding with my dad.

As you move through the years and the stories, remember the following observation by Pro Football Hall of Fame football coach, Tony Dungy:

"a mentor is someone who reaches out to help someone along the path of life"

It really is that simple. We ALL have it in us. That's what my life experience has shown me.

The author - March 1966 - 9 years old

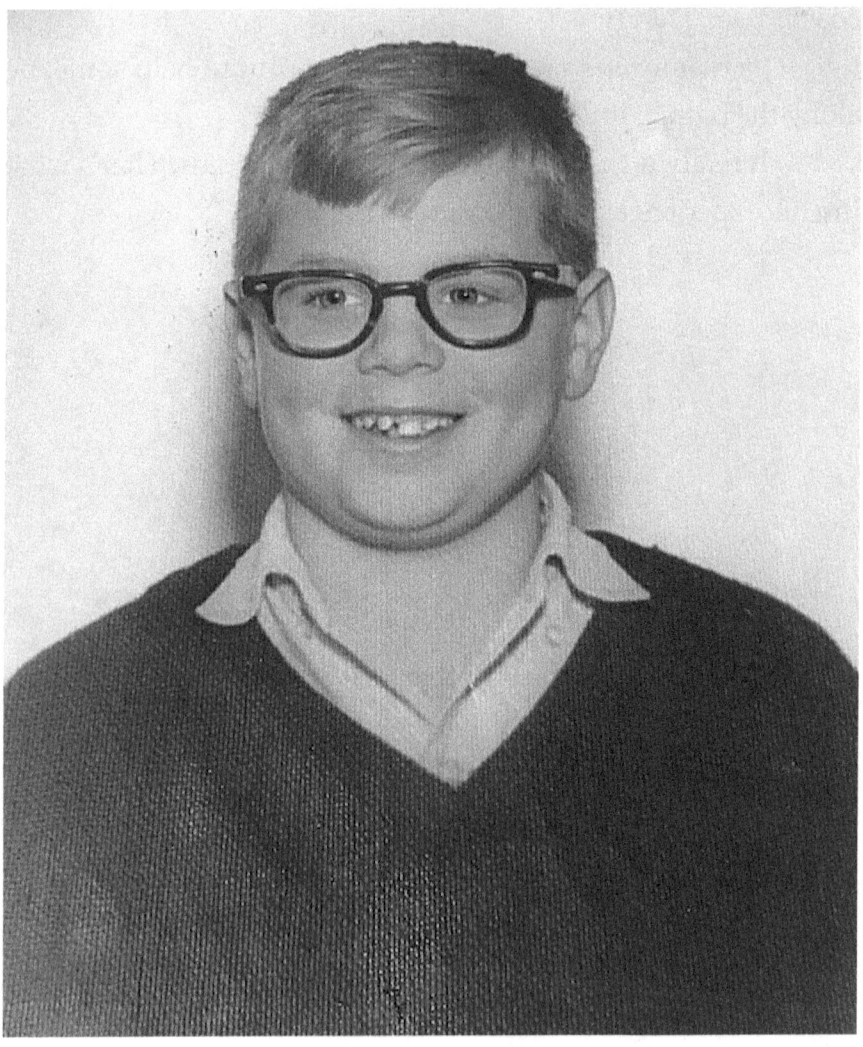

2

Mike Keville

"True heroism is remarkably sober, very undramatic. It is not the urge to surpass all others at whatever cost, but the urge to serve others at whatever the cost."

Arthur Ashe

"People may not remember exactly what you did or what you said, but they will always remember how you made them feel."

Maya Angelou

I was only 9 years old when I was willingly thrust into a new environment. Some might think of it as a fraternity of sorts, but I think tribe might be a more accurate description of the world I entered. The tribe was the oceanfront lifeguards of the Virginia Beach Patrol (VBP), and the environment was an all-male collection of teens and young men, each overflowing with testosterone and all things masculine. That first day, in early June of 1966, I was excited, yet nervous about what awaited me. I had no idea what to expect. But when my brother Jimmy and I arrived at the lifeguard shack that morning I found myself in the midst of a tribe of tanned gods and immediately longed to be one of them.

"Hey Jimmy, is that your munchkin?" The question came from one of the other lifeguards, a skinny guy with zinc oxide on his nose to protect it from sunburn.

"Yeah, this is my little brother, Shep," said Jimmy, "he's gonna be my helper this year."

"Really?" said the skinny guy, "How old is he?"

Did he not see me standing right next to Jimmy? As the youngest in my clan, I was used to people sometimes talking about me as though I wasn't standing right in front of them, but it still pissed me off.

"He's nine," said Jimmy.

I quickly added, with emphasis, "nine and a HALF!"

The other guy just smirked and remarked, "riiiiight!"

As he turned to go bother someone else Jimmy gave me the look that said, "Yeah, he's an asshole so don't worry about it."

I stuck close to Jimmy that first morning and took my cues from him. Even so, I was drinking it all in, and each morning that followed I would watch the whole scene with boundless curiosity. Those early morning meetings were always held in the small parking lot adjacent to the lifeguard shack and guys would arrive by various means of transportation. Some drove, some car-pooled, some rode bikes or motorcycles and some even walked. Inevitably, a handful straggled in late and would immediately be on the receiving end of a large dose of verbal abuse from the "responsible" ones who had shown up on time.

It was not at all unusual to hear things like, "Thanks for showing up George! Late night? Hope she was worth it." I always wondered what the "it" was that defined her worth.

Anyway, there never seemed to be a shortage of chatter amongst the tribe of lifeguards. Inevitably, the comments would again turn to the previous night's activities, who got "lucky" and who didn't, who's girlfriend was hot and who's wasn't. There was always a good amount of boasting and verbal jousting and while I hadn't a clue as to what most of it meant, I still soaked it up. This, I thought, is how real guys are. It was exactly the kind of thing I needed to be learning at that point in my life, or so I thought.

Just then I heard someone shout, "Jimmy J!"

I turned to see who it was. That's when I first laid eyes on Mike Keville.

"Hey Mike," said Jimmy, "come over and meet my little bro."

If you think about it, there really is no template for heroes.

They can come in all shapes and sizes and appear when you least expect it. I didn't know it that first day, but Mike Keville would turn out to be my very first hero. He wasn't a part of my life for very long, roughly about six weeks. But the impact he made on me in that short period was indelible. That's exactly the kind of impact heroes can have on us.

Mike stuck out his hand and said, "Hey Shep, I'm Mike Keville." I grabbed his hand and gave it as firm of a shake as I could. "Jimmy told me you were gonna be his helper this year."

I nodded without saying anything but somehow, I knew right away that Mike was not like the skinny guy. It's been over 50 years since Mike Keville became a hero to me by coming to my "rescue" during that summer in 1966. But I remember it like it was yesterday.

The city of Virginia Beach encompasses 497 square miles of land. In 1966, the majority of that land was agricultural and most of the 137,500 residents lived somewhat close to the resort area at the oceanfront. While the winters were a very slow time in the city, by the time summer rolled around, Virginia Beach came alive with tourists and lots of activity around the oceanfront.

Beginning in the early 1930's, lifeguards manned the resort beaches every summer, keeping watch over swimmers. The summer of '66 was the second summer my oldest brother Jimmy worked as a lifeguard for the Virginia Beach Patrol. At 9 years old and 11 years his junior, I'd had very few opportunities to spend any quality time with Jimmy in my short life. When he was a high school freshman, it was decided he would go away to boarding school in Maryland. I was only 2 years old at the time. After graduating from high school in 1964, he enrolled at Hampden-Sydney College and by the summer of '66 he had finished his sophomore year. Although I looked up to him the way I'm sure most younger brothers do to their older brothers, I barely knew him. But in the summer of 1966, all that was about to change.

The Virginia Beach Patrol (VBP) was owned and operated by Hugh Kitchin and Graham Hinnant, two long time Virginia Beach residents and former lifeguards themselves from the early days. These two men, who everybody knew as "Hugh Boy" and "Dusty", also owned the Umbrella Beach Service (UBS), which provided the beach chairs, umbrellas and floats the lifeguards would rent to beachgoers every day. Although the oceanfront in Virginia Beach extends from Cape Henry at the mouth of the Chesapeake Bay, south to the North Carolina border, roughly 28 miles, only three miles of that was covered by lifeguards each summer. Those three miles of beach are known as the resort area and in those forty blocks, separated from the beach by a concrete boardwalk, was every form of hotel, motel, cottage, restaurant, amusement park: anything catering to tourists.

Early that summer, our mom thought it would be great to find a way to get me, the youngest of her four children, out of the house (and out of her hair!). As it turned out, the plan she and dad devised would end up being a life changer for me. It was pretty simple really: I would go to work with Jimmy every day and be his "helper." I'm not sure I can adequately express the euphoria I felt upon hearing the news. As the youngest of 4 in my family, I was very often left out of much of the cool stuff my older siblings got to do. Mom always said my day would come and this time, maybe she was right! I was so stoked! And Jimmy? Not so much, but he did agree that I could be of some help to him. What I didn't know then was that I was the least of his worries that summer.

That first day and every morning thereafter, Jimmy and I would hop on his Honda Sport 50 motorcycle, (no helmets, mind you) and head south from our home on 58th Street. Although Jimmy's Honda Sport 50 was only one step up from a moped, I didn't care. I was embarking on the first great adventure of my life and in my mind, it was a Harley-Davidson hog and Jimmy and I were just a couple of bad-ass guys heading to work. The only things missing from my fantasy were flowing gold locks blowing in the wind, aviator sunglasses and a fu-manchu mustache!

Our destination each morning was the lifeguard shack on 18th Street where the entire contingent of lifeguards, probably close to 50 guys, would muster at the beginning of each day. Although I grew up in a house of mostly males (in addition to Jimmy, there was my dad, and my brother Fred), I had never experienced anything quite like those early morning meetings of the lifeguards. Without a doubt, I thought it was the coolest thing I had ever experienced. I mean, all the lifeguards were worthy of worship as far as I was concerned. Sun tanned gods who surfed, partied hard and still worked 7 days a week, sun-up to sun-down. They were oceanfront royalty. Deep within my young male soul, I had a longing to be just like them. No, I actually wanted to be one of them! I wanted to be part of the tribe.

The early morning meeting was the only time of the day the whole tribe was together, other than the weekly "drill." Once announcements were over, the tribe would break up and head out to their respective streets to start their long day.

In the early part of the summer of '66, Jimmy was assigned to the beach at 10th Street. In those days, it was typical for the life-guards who didn't have junior guards working with them to use unofficial "helpers." Like me, these were guys who were not yet old enough to be junior guards (you had to be at least 15). Most of these "helpers" lived close to the oceanfront and were somewhere in the neighborhood of 12 to 14 years old which meant, compared to my 9 and a half, I was once again low man in the pecking order. While they had nothing to do with the lifesaving aspect of the lifeguard responsibilities, the "helpers" did provide a valuable service: manual labor. Back then, not only were the lifeguards charged with protecting swimmers, but they were also responsible for renting umbrellas, beach chairs, and floats to beachgoers every day. This is where the "helpers" proved their worth.

There were only two parts of any day that could be considered physically rigorous for the lifeguards of the VBP: set up and takedown. It stands to reason the only way to really entice someone to rent anything was to have it already set up and ready to go. So, every morning, once they arrived at their respective streets, the lifeguards, junior lifeguards, and the unofficial helpers, would go about the task of unpacking their allotment of chairs, umbrellas and floats, haul them roughly 30 yards down to the beach from the boardwalk and begin setting them up. At the end of each day, around 5:30 pm, they would take everything down, haul it back to the boardwalk, pack it up and cover it with a thick canvas tarp until the next morning. Doesn't sound like all that much in this day and age of aluminum, lightweight fabric, and boogie boards. In 1966 however, everything was made with wood, canvas and thick rubber.

Set up had to be precise. The canvas umbrellas were either blue, green or yellow and had to be arranged in the same repeating pattern on every street. The green colored floats were stacked under an umbrella next to the yellow lifeguard stand. Chairs were blue and white canvas on an oak frame; and two were positioned underneath each umbrella.

In my desperate quest to be seen as one of the tribe, I worked very hard trying to carry as many heavy chairs and bulky umbrellas as I could during set up and take down. Jimmy and Mike Keville, who was on the next street to the south, took the time to teach me the techniques used to make carrying the heavy chairs and umbrellas easier. Try as I might, I would usually just end up slowing things down because I wasn't yet strong enough. So, I was set to the task of moving all of the lighter weight floats down to their spot on the beach and then bringing them back to the boardwalk at the end of the day.

It was understood by all the lifeguards that the number of umbrellas and chairs you set up on your street was a good indication of the importance of your street in terms of rentals. Whether you had a lot to set up or not depended on one thing only: the kind of hotel or motel that was on your street. This, in turn, also determined whether a street had two lifeguards assigned or just one.

There wasn't a large hotel on 10th Street back in '66. Consequently, 10th Street was not considered a big producer in terms of rentals, so Jimmy was the sole guard assigned. As his "helper" I was in nine-year-old boy's heaven, and I actually got "paid" for my efforts. That is, I got to choose the best float out of our allotment of floats, and I was allowed to use it for free all day long! Or at least until it was take down time. Who needed money when you had a choice of floats for the whole day?

Before the advent of the Morey boogie board in the early '70s, the wave riding vehicle of choice was called a surf mat, raft or float but they were all pretty much made the same way: an inflatable rubber core covered by thick cotton canvas. They came in various sizes and were almost always rectangular in some dimension.

Like everything else, some floats were of better quality than others. Even at nine and half years of age, I knew my floats and the Umbrella Beach Service had the best floats I had ever seen. You could inflate UBS floats to the point they would be very rigid and would maintain that level of rigidity. They rarely leaked any air. They were a nine-year-old surfer wannabe's dream. All of the cool older guys were surfers and I wanted to be a surfer, too. Jimmy had a sweet Hobie board but our mom, who would let me ride a motorcycle with no helmet, denied my desire to actually use a real surfboard for fear I would somehow get hurt or maybe even drown. That didn't matter because I soon realized I was small enough so that I could kneel on my rigid Umbrella Beach Service float, catch waves and quickly get to my feet and "surf" to the shore. I hardly ever came out of the water that summer.

Virginia Beach was still a small city back in '66 and most of the lifeguards either knew each other or knew of each other from local gossip and legend. Like any tribe, there was a pecking order that was determined by predictable characteristics: how old you were, how many years you had been a lifeguard, who your family was and how cool you were perceived to be. By that criteria Jimmy was pretty high in the tribe's pecking order and so by association only I was acceptable, albeit invisible, to the rest of the lifeguards.

Since the only time all the lifeguards were together each day was at the early morning meeting, once you got to your assigned street, the only other lifeguards you came into contact with during the day were the ones within a block or two of your street.

Neither Jimmy nor I remember the name of the lifeguard who manned 11th Street to our north so I'm going to refer to him as "Mr. Pottymouth." The guy was pretty surly and, as my mom used to say, looked like "something the cat dragged in." Every lifeguard wore a pair of custom-made, navy-blue canvas trunks with the letters, "VBP" in contrasting white on the right thigh. Mr. Pottymouth's trunks were constantly in a state of disrepair. They were faded beyond belief and sometimes with a letter or two of the "VBP" missing or hanging by a thread. I'm not sure if he ever combed his dark hair which gave him that just rolled out of bed look every day.

What I remember the most though is that he had a pretty loose reign on his language. Even at 9 years old and with two older brothers I'd never heard the F-bomb until Mr. Pottymouth. He used it frequently and in various grammatical forms. In fact, he was so proficient in his use of vocabulary of the same nature that in no time at all I learned a whole bunch of what I initially believed to be cool new words.

But it would drive Jimmy nuts whenever Mr. Pottymouth let fly because not only did I hear it, but also any nearby tourists. I soon realized these were words I shouldn't be using especially since I wasn't altogether sure what any of them meant!

What bothered Jimmy the most was how Mr. Pottymouth's looks, and language reflected badly on the group of lifeguards, teaching me that what you say and how you present yourself does matter. I never liked Mr. Pottymouth anyway. Somehow, I knew his was not the example I should try to follow. I'm sure he was a good guy underneath, but we steered clear of him as much as possible. Jimmy had more in common and a better connection with the guys to our south on 9th and 8th streets. On 9th Street, one block to our south, was Mike Keville's domain.

But then, there was Clancy, one of the lieutenants of the Virginia Beach Patrol. Clancy probably had a last name but, like Cher, Bono and Prince, he really didn't need one. Along with the handful of other lieutenants, Clancy basically rode up and down the boardwalk all day long in a white Jeep pickup truck, keeping an eye on things.

But Clancy wasn't like the other lieutenants. He was a little older, probably late thirties or maybe even early 40's. The thing that struck me the most when I first encountered Clancy that summer was his tan. It was only early June and yet he already had a deep, mid-summer tan. I later learned that Clancy "wintered" in Florida each year doing who knows what.

The other thing I found peculiar was in all my time being Jimmy's helper (there were two more summers after '66) I never once saw Clancy without sunglasses on...ever. There could be a Nor'easter blowing, totally overcast and raining: he would still have his shades on. Clancy may have had teeth; I wouldn't know because I never saw the guy smile. He wore a perpetual, intimi-dating scowl. Not to mention that when he happened to look my way it was with a "who the hell are you" kinda look. Even with his shades on, I could tell that's what he was thinking!

One day I finally asked Jimmy, "Why does Clancy always have his sunglasses on?"

Jimmy pondered for a minute and, trying to come up with something that would make sense to a nine-year-old and offered, "Well, maybe it's because he usually stays out late most nights."

I wasn't altogether certain why staying out late would demand Clancy's constant use of sunglasses, but I decided to keep quiet and not annoy Jimmy with continued interrogation.

As much as I was intrigued by guys like Clancy and Mr. Pottymouth, from that very first morning, I just knew Mike Keville was the better role model. And I was soon to find out that my intuition was right.

Mike was a Virginia Beach native and loved everything about the beach: the ocean, the waves, surfing and the sand between his toes. He was an Eagle Scout in his youth, and as a member of the Class of '65 at the old Virginia Beach High School, he was heavily involved with school activities and sports, playing football, basketball and running track.

Mike put his athletic ability and competitive spirit on display every Friday afternoon at the weekly drill session. The drill was created by Hugh Boy and Dusty and was designed to ensure their lifeguards remained in good shape. Similar to modern day triathlons (without the bike), the drill seemed to me to be very grueling.

The entire tribe of lifeguards would start out on the beach and sprint to the ocean to begin a 100-yard swim out to a buoy that had been placed by one of the lieutenants. Once they made it to the buoy, they would turn and begin swimming north, parallel to the beach, to the next buoy which was about a quarter of a mile away. Rounding that buoy, they'd swim the 100 yards back to the beach. Once they reached the beach they'd have to run, in the deep sand, back to the original starting point a quarter of a mile away.

The drill wasn't a competition per se. But each lifeguard had to complete it. Most of the guys complained about having to do it and for the vast majority of lifeguards, finishing was their only goal. Nevertheless, no one wanted to be bringing up the rear either. Jimmy's approach was to be in the middle of the pack. That way you reduced the risk of being kicked or jostled by another lifeguard and you could complete the drill without incident.

For a handful however, the weekly drill was a full-on competitive event. One of that handful was Mike Keville. I soon learned the only question during drill each week was who would come in first, Mike or Tim Wood. Wanting to get the best vantage point, I would head up to the boardwalk from the beach as the lifeguards began their initial sprint to the sea. I would keep my eye on Jimmy of course but inevitably my focus returned to the front of the pack where I would always find Mike, Tim, and maybe a couple of others. I marveled not only at Mike and Tim's ability but also their competitive drive. Once the front of the pack began leaving the ocean to begin their final sprint, I would run back down to the finish line on the beach to cheer them on.

Regardless of who was first, one thing was always evident between Mike and Tim: mutual respect. Never once did I see a hint of boastful behavior from either of them. It was more like an unspoken appreciation of bringing out the best in each other. For the first time in my life, I witnessed what would take me years to fully understand: most males have a deep need to be perceived as competent, able, and worthy of respect; maybe even more so than the need to feel loved. I learned that one sure way to earn and gain respect is to do your very best in every situation and be humble, like Mike and Tim, no matter the outcome.

Actually, Mike had every reason to be "too cool for school": lean and athletic with boyishly good looks and sandy brown hair made blond by the sun, he was, by all accounts, a sensitive, loyal and thoughtful person. Mike clearly loved life and found enjoyment in even the simplest of activities.

Always upbeat and smiling, Mike had a place in his heart

for young kids, too. From that first morning, Mike treated me like, well, one of the guys, part of the tribe. Not a day went by that he didn't talk with me; see how I was doing. He didn't have to do that and frankly most of the other lifeguards barely noticed that I even existed. But not Mike. Without a doubt, he was one of the most likable people I've ever known.

By the summer of '66, Mike had finished his first year at Virginia Tech, where he was majoring in Biology. My lifelong bond with him was cast in stone one day early that July.

It was getting close to lunchtime. Jimmy and I had not packed a lunch that day so Jimmy decided he would grab us a couple of hotdogs from Grumpy's, a well-known restaurant/bar a block away on the corner of 9th and Atlantic Avenue. Anytime a lifeguard working solo (like Jimmy) needed to go grab lunch or take a quick bathroom break, he would signal the guards on the streets adjacent to them and those guards would cover while he was gone. So, when Jimmy yelled out to me (I was in the water of course) that he was going to pick up lunch, I knew we were covered.

Every lifeguard on the Beach knew that the one thing most likely to cause trouble for swimmers in the ocean is a phenomenon known as rip currents. Rip currents take shape as the water from waves crashing up on the shore finds its way back out to sea. Water will naturally seek the easiest route and it's the contour of the ocean floor that dictates where rip currents form. So, beaches that are rocky or have a coral bottom will be very predictable as the contours are basically fixed. Virginia Beach is a sand beach though, so the bottom contour is constantly undergoing change due to ocean currents and waves. Consequently, the location of rip currents can change daily.

The best way to envision rip currents is to imagine them as underwater rivers. Sandbars that form underwater are like the banks of the river. They are the high spots and will slow the movement of water back out to sea. In some spots, though, where there is no sandbar, water will funnel through that opening and move quickly and sometimes forcefully, like a river, back out to sea. Many an unsuspecting swimmer has been lost after being caught in a rip current. I was somewhat familiar with rip currents but this was a relatively calm day with not a lot of big wave action.

Completely obsessed with surfing, I was nevertheless out there on my "pick of the litter" float, catching whatever I could. What I didn't fully understand then was that my obsession was in large part due to my search for an identity. I just knew that I wanted to be seen as one of the tribe but to do that, I had to look and act like one of its members. Consequently, being an accomplished waterman was part of the identity. I couldn't take part in the drill and I couldn't carry the heavy chairs or umbrellas. So, surfing on my float each day was the only thing I could do to prove my worth. But I loved every bit of it; being in the water, catching waves and feeling the exhilaration of standing and riding waves to the beach.

Not long after Jimmy left for Grumpy's, I caught a small wave and rode it all the way to the shoreline. Thinking I was done with the wave, I relaxed and prepared to step off my float on to the beach. Suddenly, another wave came up from behind and knocked the float out from underneath me. I went head over heels and landed squarely on my tailbone.

"Damn it all" I said (a phrase I had recently learned from Mr. Pottymouth!) In my moment of pain and embarrassment I lost track of my float. Only when I managed to get to my feet and look around did I notice: my float, which was not really mine but the Umbrella Beach Service's float, Hugh Kitchin's and Dusty Hinnant's float--the one my brother was ultimately responsible for that he'd let me use--was heading straight out to sea! By the time I had gotten up, the float had been carried back to the ocean and into a subtle, yet strong rip current. It was at least 20 yards offshore and showing no signs of slowing down.

Something happens when outright panic seizes control of a nine-year old's body. I wouldn't say that my life flashed before my eyes when I realized my Umbrella Beach Service float was heading straight out to the open ocean. I mean, at that point I really didn't have much life to be flashed. But in an instant, time seemed to stand still as all else in the universe lost focus. And yet, my mind immediately went into warp speed.

I quickly determined I wasn't a strong enough swimmer to try and retrieve my float from the rip current so that option was eliminated. I was facing 11th street and I looked at the life-guard stand: Mr. Pottymouth was nowhere in sight. Not that he would have done anything had he noticed what was happening. I quickly turned to 9th street: I didn't see Mike or his junior guard, Jonny Sedel. When I turned back to see where my float was, I noticed there was this fat guy only about 5 yards away from it, right on the edge of the rip current. Surely, he would come to my rescue!

So, I yelled to him, "Hey, mister, can you grab my float?!"

I was certain he could see my distress and fully under-stood the consequences for me if he didn't come to my rescue. Until the day I die, I will never forget the expression on this guy's face as he looked back at me after watching my float go right by him, making absolutely no effort to grab it. Without saying a word his look basically said, "Dude, you are so screwed."

He was my last hope.

In that moment I just knew it: my life was over. If there had been a hole to crawl in to, I would have done just that. Instead, I stood there at the shoreline, my mind ablaze with the multitude of negative consequences and embarrassment I knew would come my way for having lost a float.

What bothered me the most though, was in my desperate and constant need to be seen and considered as one of the tribe, this one screw-up would make it crystal clear to everyone that I, in fact, didn't have what it takes. I didn't measure up. I was crushed.

It wasn't until the last second of my moment of complete devastation at the shoreline that I noticed, out of the corner of my eye, that Mike Keville was sprinting up the beach towards me. He was on me and by me in a flash, just like Superman. As he dove into the surf in front of me and started stroking powerfully out to sea, my heart filled with excitement and relief. Mike was going to rescue my float and save the day for me!

You can't imagine what a thing of as beauty it was to watch this athletic guy tear through the rip current as if it were nothing. Once he caught up to my wayward float, he hopped on and started to paddle in.

The fat guy just watched.

Just as quickly, my exhilaration and relief turned to complete dread. If there was one person on the entire Virginia Beach Patrol staff (other than Jimmy of course) whose opinion of me mattered more than anything else, it was Mike Keville. And here he comes after saving my butt from a huge screw up. My mind raced: what am I gonna say? Surely he will be disgusted and understandably annoyed at having to come to the rescue of a little twerp who can't even take care of his own float. Knowing the kind of guy Mike was though, I'm surprised I had that thought at all.

From the moment Mike sprinted by me until the time he paddled back in, I don't think I moved a millimeter. I was frozen. As he walked up to me with my rebellious float under his arm I opened my mouth as if to say something but nothing came out. Mike just smiled that killer smile of his, handed me my float and said, "Here you go buddy; try to hang on to this thing!"

And, just like that, it was over.

My mom used to always say to me at such times, "If this is the worst thing that ever happens to you, you'll be lucky."

She was right, of course, but at that moment in time, it <u>was</u> the worst thing that had ever happened to me. The whole episode had probably taken only a matter of minutes but to me it seemed like an eternity.

As Mike began to walk back to his lifeguard stand on 9th street, my ability to speak miraculously returned and I muttered a feeble, "Thanks Mike." I didn't know what else to say and "thanks" didn't seem nearly enough but it was all I had. I'm not even sure he heard me. Right then, Mike Keville became a hero to me. Before I knew it, Jimmy was back with our hot dogs.

"Everything OK?" he asked.

The rest of that day was a blur. I don't even remember eating my Grumpy's hot dog. I suppose I may have been in a state of shock to some degree but it was probably more like a state of awe at what Mike had done for me. I did all I could to act as normal as possible the rest of that day; I didn't want to let on that anything unusual had taken place. For a split second, the fear that Mike might tell everybody what had happened crossed my mind. But just as quickly I came to my senses; that's just not who he was.

Not long after that fateful day Jimmy (with me in tow) was transferred to the lifeguard stand at 25th street. Everything changed. Not that 10th street was all that slow but moving to 25th Street was like going to Manhattan from Mayberry. Set up and take down of chairs and umbrellas doubled to accommodate folks staying at the old Breakers Hotel to the south and the newer Princess Anne Inn to the north. We gained a junior guard, a great guy named Sparky Hathaway, who Jimmy has stayed in contact with over the years. We were there the rest of that summer as well as the summer of '67. I rarely saw much of Mike again after we moved up to 25th street.

Although I didn't know it at the time, the summer of '66 proved to be a pivotal time for Jimmy. Having recently completed his sophomore year at Hampden-Sydney College, the school informed him that although he had not failed any classes, he would not be allowed to return for the fall semester. He had fallen victim to the "sophomore slump" and the school was uncertain as to the level of his motivation for higher education. They felt a semester off might help him figure that out. Normally that wouldn't be a serious issue but in the summer of 1966 the Vietnam conflict was heating up and any young man not enrolled in college was subject to being called up to military service. So, he decided to join the Marines as a reservist and shipped off to Parris Island, S.C. as the summer ended that September. Years later he confided in me that being one of the lifeguards that year really helped him prepare for boot camp. Being a part of the close-knit brotherhood of lifeguards helped him to stay focused and the weekly drills helped keep him in shape.

As Jimmy headed off to Marine Corps boot camp that September, Mike headed back to Virginia Tech to start his sophomore year. His life was also about to change in a big way.

It started at a party. Mike's best friend, Tom Parks, had a girlfriend, Susan, who was at the party also. Seems that Susan had a new roommate, Shirley Hodges, whom she had brought to the party.

As Shirley puts it, "I saw Mike across a crowded room and asked Susan who he was. It turned out to be her boyfriend's best friend. I asked her to introduce me. We danced the night away and that weekend we went to the first football game of the year. We were never apart after that."

Mike and Shirley were married on June 29, 1968, the summer before their final year at Virginia Tech.

In the forty years following the summer of '66, Jimmy and I continued down our separate paths, and I completely lost track of Mike. In 1967, I spent 3 weeks away at Camp Greenbrier in West Virginia and in 1968 I spent the whole summer there. Jimmy completed his Marine Corps training in November of '66 and made his way back to Hampden-Sydney to finish his degree. He continued to lifeguard and when I wasn't away at camp, I'd head to the oceanfront with him just as I had in 1966. Jimmy's lifeguard days came to an end in 1970 and by then I had started going to a daily sports camp at Norfolk Academy. Ironic, I suppose, that as much as I had at one time wanted so desperately to be a lifeguard, I never actually became one.

It was only many years later, probably around 2008, that Mike Keville's name came up in conversation. Jimmy and I had started a Saturday morning ritual of having breakfast together at a place called the Beach Pub in Virginia Beach. It had literally been a lifetime since that magical summer of 1966.

One Saturday morning on our way to breakfast, we passed a small house that we had passed countless times before. The house has been there as long as I can remember and today it's the home of a seafood store. But, at some point early in its history the house had been a residence.

Out of the blue Jimmy asked me, "Hey, you remember Mike Keville?"

I hadn't heard Mike's name in decades, but the mere mention of his name immediately brought a smile to my face.

"You bet I do," I said, "why do you ask?"

"That was his house," Jimmy said as he pointed to the seafood store.

My mind immediately began to drift back to the summer of '66, to the cast of characters and especially that day Mike came to my rescue.

"Mike was just the greatest guy," I said, "whatever happened to him?"

Jimmy hesitated for a second and, as I looked over at him, I could see the emotion on his face.

He said, "Well, he got testicular cancer and died in 1970."

As I sat there in stunned silence, we pulled into the Pub parking lot. I had no idea. How did I not know? Turns out we ended up talking a lot about our friend Mike Keville during breakfast that morning.

Mike and Shirley had much to look forward to in 1969. They would both graduate from Virginia Tech in June and begin the next chapter of their lives together. The Vietnam conflict had escalated into a full-on war by then and young men all over the country were being called up to serve. Mike had a notion that he would like to be a Naval Aviator but had to settle for Navigator due to his eyesight. In February of that year Mike went to the doctor because he was concerned about a lump that had formed on his testicle. Thinking it was likely just a broken blood vessel the doctor said there was no reason for concern.

A month later, Mike went back to the same doctor, this time for a physical, which was required for his application to the Aviation Officer Program of the U.S. Navy. Although the lump had gotten larger, the doctor once again told Mike it was nothing to worry about. And so, he didn't.

Mike finished his classes in early April and officially joined the U.S. Naval Air Reserve. While he waited for his aviation program to start, he took a job as an Inspector at the Food & Drug Administration in Baltimore, Maryland.

Mike and Shirley graduated together in June of 1969 and came to visit family in Virginia Beach for a few days before heading back to Baltimore. As fate would have it, Mike went surfing one of those days and after wiping out on a wave, his board hit him squarely in groin area. He was in a bit of pain and Shirley convinced him to go see a doctor but this time, she wanted him to see a urologist. And so, he did.

On June 13, 1969, just a couple of weeks shy of their first wedding anniversary, Mike went to the doctor. Three days later, on June 16, Mike had his first surgery to have his testicle removed.

It was malignant.

Not long after, he had a second surgery to remove as many lymph nodes as possible and they then returned to Baltimore. As the world welcomed in a new year and new decade in January of 1970, Mike had a sense that the cancer had come back. He was right. After exploratory surgery revealed it had spread throughout his body, Mike began a brutal regimen of experimental chemotherapy drugs. Nothing seemed to make an impact and Mike finally decided he'd had enough. He passed on May 18th, 1970. He was only 22 years old.

Why does it seem to hit us harder when a young person dies before their time? Especially someone like Mike Keville who had so much to offer this world. I can tell you that's exactly what I was thinking that morning after learning Mike had passed away so many years ago, in the prime of his life.

Jimmy and I reminisced about the summer of '66 during breakfast. All the cast of characters and the changes brought about by our move to 25th street halfway through the summer. We laughed about Clancy (turns out everybody was intimidated by Clancy!). We even tried to remember Mr. Pottymouth's real name but couldn't.

Predictably, the conversation kept coming back to Mike. Something was really nagging at me but I couldn't quite put my finger on it.

I took the opportunity to finally reveal to Jimmy how Mike had saved my butt that day while he was off getting us hot dogs at Grumpy's. Turns out my faith that Mike would keep the story just between us was well placed. Jimmy had no idea and was quick to point out that characteristics like that are exactly why he, too, thought so much of Mike.

Still, something else was nagging me.

Strange as it may seem, I eventually realized that what was nagging me was simply a feeling of grief. I was feeling a deep sense of sadness from learning that Mike had died a young man.

I'd known and interacted with Mike Keville every day for only 6 weeks way back in 1966. That's just 42 days. Yet, a little over 40 years later, I found myself grieving over losing him at such a young age. How could that be?

It took me a while to understand why.

We all need heroes in our lives and that's especially true for young males. We need the kind of people we can look up to and know, deep down in our souls, that they set the example we should try to live by. People who show us through their words and actions how to live life honorably, with courage, faith and humility. People who don't ask or look for praise and recognition. The ones who help simply because it's the right thing to do, not because of the muted thank you they receive doing a kindness. People, who will always have our backs when we need it the most.

That's exactly the kind of person Mike Keville was, and I grieved because frankly, there aren't enough people like that in the world anymore.

Mike had such great potential as a human being. It saddened me to think about the loss of the positive impact he could have made on so many other lives, just as he had on mine in just 6 short weeks.

I'm not sure if Mike ever considered what his legacy would be. Most likely, he didn't live long enough to think about things like that. But I know this: I am a part of Mike Keville's legacy and I still grieve to this day because I never got the chance to tell him what a hero he had been to me. I never got a chance to thank him. Not just for coming to my rescue that fateful day, but more importantly, for selflessly going out of his way to make me, a twerpy little nine-year-old kid, feel like I really mattered, like I belonged…like I was part of the tribe. And when I needed it, Mike had my back.

It only takes a second to make a positive impact that lasts a lifetime. Mike Keville taught me that when I was only 9 (and a half!) years old. I've never forgotten his example.

He's still a hero to me.

At his request, Michael Francis Keville was laid to rest in a secluded spot on 200 acres owned by Shirley's family. Its peaceful there.

By faith, I know that one bright day I will see Mike again, hopefully on a beach somewhere with a beautiful sunrise and sand between my toes. I will tell him then how grateful I was for his example and what he meant to me in this life. And then I'm sure we'll have a good laugh about the day he saved my butt!

Mike Keville – Virginia Beach Oceanfront - 1967

3

Dave Boettger

"Not looking to your own interests but each of you to the interests of the others."

Philippians 2:4

"Nothing in the world is worth having or worth doing unless it means effort, pain, difficulty...I have never in my life envied a human being who led an easy life. I have envied a great many people who led difficult lives and led them well."

Theodore Roosevelt

26th President of the United States

The following summer of 1967 my brother Jimmy once again manned the lifeguard stand on 25th street but it would be mid-July before I joined back up with him. That's because in early June, I left home for the first time in my life and embarked on a new adventure. I was genuinely excited because deep down, I think most males crave the idea of adventure; it's woven into our DNA. What appeals to us is that adventure requires a degree of risk; of willingly sticking one's neck out to discover what we're made of, to see if we have what it takes. At 10 years old, that wasn't something I had ever done. To be honest, I was somewhat of a mama's boy but that was about to change.

My destination was Camp Greenbrier (CG), an all-boys overnight camp in the sleepy little nowhere town of Alderson, West Virginia. Other than the handful of times I'd spent the night at a friend's house in the neighborhood, I had yet to be away from the security and comfort of my own home and bed for any length of time. I did find a degree of comfort in knowing that a good number of my friends from school were also going to camp, but I was nevertheless a little apprehensive about what lay ahead. How would I measure up?

In 1967 the quickest and most efficient mode of transportation to camp was via passenger train. Alderson is a quaint little town nestled in the Appalachian foothills of the southeastern part of the state. It currently boasts about 1000 permanent residents and, of course, a train station. On the morning of departure for camp, campers and their families from our area gathered at the Norfolk and Western train station in Norfolk, Virginia. As we checked in and waited for the call to board the train, parents chatted politely while campers tried to control their nervous anticipation about the adventure ahead. Finally, the time came to board and after saying our goodbyes we all piled on to the passenger cars to begin the long journey west. There would be multiple stops along the way, most notably in Richmond, Va. where we picked up another group of campers and counselors.

The first half of the trip was exactly what you might expect from a mob of prepubescent and fully pubescent boys: totally raucous. The handful of counselors making the trip to supervise us had their hands full, but we didn't care. We were free from parental bondage and the feeling of liberation was intoxicating! The spaciousness of the passenger car provided us ease of movement so very few boys stayed in one place for long. 'Pods" of boys would form throughout the car, talking about everything from baseball to girls, and then they would break up, move on and new pods would form.

At some point, I found myself in a pod consisting of new campers like me and two veteran campers, David and Steve. David and Steve were holding court for us newbies and proceeded to give us the lowdown about the important things at camp, like the food.

"Oh yeah," said Steve, "the food is to die for. I love the breakfasts. You can smell it even before you get to the Mess Hall! They're just the best."

"I like the bug juice we get at lunch and dinner," said David. "It's so good after a hot day."

For the uninitiated, "bug juice" is another name for Kool Aid, the popular drink mix back then. It was simply artificial fruit flavoring combined with water and a lot of sugar, but it sure tasted good when you were hot and sweaty. We were told the name "bug juice" comes from the fact that, courtesy of the ample amount of sugar in the drink, bugs liked it too and if you let your bug juice sit unattended for very long, well, the bugs would show up to get a drink.

All of that was fascinating to me but I was interested in something else. "Who's your favorite counselor?" I asked neither in particular.

"I like Lee Smoot," said David without hesitation, "I think he's the head of Junior Camp this year. He's been coming to camp a long time and he's really a nice guy."

"I like Lee, too," Steve added, "but honestly, I would say all the counselors at camp are good guys." David nodded in agreement.

Steve continued, "I mean you've got DP (real name Dennis Pruitt), Jeff Steckroth, Jay Bowen, Lester Wilson, Bill Compton just to mention a few; all those guys are cool, too."

David broke in, "and don't forget Dave!'

At that Steve rolled his eyes and proclaimed, "God help you if Dave is your baseball coach!"

I knew Steve was referring to Dave Boettger (pronounced Bet-ger). Just like the other guys they mentioned, I'd heard Dave's name alluded to during the school year by some of the other veteran campers. Everyone liked him but all agreed there was a part of Dave which validated Steve's proclamation. Dave Boettger, I'd heard, did not like to lose at anything. Didn't matter what the competition was, big or small, Dave hated to lose. And on those occasions where he did lose, Dave took it hard. He expected a lot out of himself and of those he coached. Deep down, I knew I needed that kind of coach. Secretly, I hoped I would be on his team. Not a minute later our pod broke up and we moved on.

As the day wore on and we continued to make our way west, things settled somewhat, and the initial excitement began to wear off. Then, without warning it seemed, the sun started to set and as night began to settle in so did a strange, terrible feeling I had never felt before: homesickness. In an instant, the mob of raucous boys slowly became very quiet as thoughts of and longings for home consumed even the most veteran campers. Watching the fire red sky out of the window after the sun had set, I could feel a lump forming in my throat. I couldn't stop thinking about home; wondering what mom had made for dinner, what was on TV and were they missing me as much as I was missing them. It took every ounce of effort not to show any hint of homesickness. As a new member of the tribe of campers, I knew that showing any sign of weakness would put an unwanted spotlight on my "rookie" status, so I did my best to appear cool with everything. I don't think I fooled anybody.

The trip seemed to take forever. I had long since eaten the food mom had sent with me and began to wonder if we would ever get to camp. Finally, around midnight, the train lumbered to a stop at the station in Alderson.

I was whipped; we all were. All the adrenaline that had fueled me earlier in the day had long ago been depleted. As we slowly disembarked from the train, I could hear camp personnel calling out camper names. The loading platform was a "beehive of activity" as counselors went about finding the campers they were responsible for. I finally heard my name from the other end of the platform so, army style duffle bag in hand, I trudged in that direction.

"Hey, are you Shep?"

As I nodded in affirmation, too tired to even say anything, Jesse Davidson stuck out his hand, "Hi, I'm Jesse, and you're gonna be in my tent. Do you know Jim?"

I did, in fact, know Jim, who had found his way to Jesse just before me. Jim Wolcott was a classmate of mine from school, so we knew each other fairly well. It was Jim's first summer at camp also and I think we were both relieved to have someone familiar in the same tent. I honestly can't remember the third camper in our tent but once Jesse had corralled all three of us, we grabbed the rest of our stuff and made our way to waiting buses. From there we began the final leg of the long journey, which would take us over the bridge on the Greenbrier River and about a mile down the road to camp. It was so dark; I could barely see anything out of the bus window as we pulled into camp. I couldn't wait to go to sleep.

I already knew a lot about CG probably because the owner at the time was also a teacher at my school. Founded in 1898, Camp Greenbrier is the oldest, privately owned summer camp in continuous operation in the United States. Located on the banks of the Greenbrier River, the camp's 35 acres provides an almost perfect landscape for its mission. The goal then as well as now is to provide an environment where boys between the ages of 7 and 15 can learn cooperation, respect, and self-confidence, all qualities a good man should have. Every aspect of camp is designed to help campers reach those goals. I got a quick taste of that early the next morning when we were awakened by reveille, yes reveille. And not just some recorded version, the real thing. Turns out one of the counselors was an accomplished trumpeter. I was honestly surprised by the early morning chill in the air which confirmed our need to bring sweatshirts to camp and served as a stark reminder that I wasn't at home in balmy Virginia Beach.

"Come on guys let's get up and get dressed," said Jesse, "leave your bunks as is, we'll take care of them after breakfast."

Just like Steve had said on the train, I could smell breakfast from the nearby Mess Hall. It smelled delicious.

Camp life was structured in somewhat of a military manner with most of the comforts of home eliminated. After about a day, however, we never missed them. There were two camp sessions every summer, each three weeks in length. Campers could come for either the first session, second session or the full term of six weeks. That first year, I was at camp for the first session only, but in the summer of 1968, I spent all six weeks there.

Camp was divided into Senior and Junior Camp depending on your age. Each camper shared a large 12'x12' heavy canvas tent with two other campers and a counselor. The tents were laid out side by side in rows, each with a heavy wooden floor set on a cinder block foundation. Tents were held up by ridge poles with two sides being secured by ropes to a post and beam running the length of either side of the tent. They had flaps on all sides that could be rolled up during the day for ventilation and rolled down at night or during bad weather.

We slept on what I believe to have been Army surplus cots which were just the right height to slide our footlockers underneath. Each tent also had a rough, wooden stand-up closet in the middle but mostly we lived out of our footlockers.

Days were tightly scheduled with activities in the mornings, followed by lunch, the requisite "rest hour" and then afternoon activities starting at 2pm each day. And the list of activities offered was the stuff a young boy dreams about. Not only were there traditional things like basketball, baseball, and tennis, but there was also swimming, canoeing, archery, riflery, camp craft, craft shop, boxing, wrestling and track. Then there were specialty activities like overnight hikes and spelunking. There truly was something for everybody.

Each camper knew that regardless of how many weeks they were at camp, the ultimate goal was to win the "Order of the Star," the highest award CG offers. Every camper had the potential to earn the award, but in order to win it, one would have to participate in as many activities as he could to earn points. If a camper were to earn at least 100 points, he would be bestowed the Order of the Star.

The three weeks of that first summer were a blur for me. Hell, it took me a good week just to get settled into the new routine! I soon realized that I would have to be super aggressive to earn enough points to earn the Order of the Star; consequently, I didn't work very hard at it.

What I did work hard at was baseball. At that time, baseball was king at CG and everyone from counselors on down to junior campers was part of a league. There were three leagues: the majors for all the counselors and a few select senior campers, the minors which closely resembled today's traditional Little League, and the coach pitch Pony League.

Another interesting twist during that era is the fact kids did not start organized sports nearly as early as they do these days. Even at 10 years old, I'd never been part of any organized league at home and only had one spring season of experience with intramural softball at school. Our softball "coach" was actually a high school student volunteering to get community service credits, so there wasn't much coaching done. Nevertheless, I was on fire for baseball. My dad and brothers Jimmy and Fred were huge baseball fans. Fred always pulled for the Yankees, but dad, Jimmy and I were die-hard Oriole fans. Both my brothers had played Little League and were known for their abilities. I had a good grasp of the rules of baseball and I was dying to be on a real team with a real coach. I wanted to be known for my abilities, too.

I frankly can't remember when I learned that I would be on Dave Boettger's team, the Wasps, but I was excited by the news. By the time I arrived at CG, Dave was already a camp legend. From Cincinnati, Ohio, he first came to CG as a camper in 1959 and then started as a Junior Counselor in 1962. Dave "retired" from camp after the 1978 session, having served in numerous leadership roles during his 16 years as a counselor. My first summer he was the Head of Senior Camp and my second summer he was the Head of Activities. Both of those jobs carried a high degree of responsibility, but I really think Dave liked being in the lead on things. It wasn't long before I, along with my fellow Wasp teammates, began our indoctrination in the Dave Boettger gospel on what it takes to be a winner.

The policy at CG back then was once you were on a team you stayed with that team the next year if you weren't ready to move up to the minor league. The same policy held true for the minor league as well. There were only two teams in the Pony League, the Wasps, and the Bees, who were coached by Lee Smoot. The rivalry was spirited and intense.

Baseball practice/games were always held at 2pm, after the post lunch, mid-day rest hour. Each league had its own field and the Pony League field was the farthest away from the tent area. The only thing farther away was the rifle range, which was roughly 30 yards beyond a large stand of tall trees that lined the first base side of our field. While the mornings at CG were typically nice and cool, by 2pm each day the heat was at peak level. Just walking out to the field would cause beads of sweat to form almost immediately. I frequently felt like I was crossing the Sahara Desert as the afternoon sun blazed and more than a few campers occasionally voiced their discomfort with the trek and the heat. The Wasps learned quickly, however, that Dave would not tolerate that kind of talk or whining of any kind, for that matter.

As the Wasps and Bees made their way out to the field for that first day of practice, all of us seemed to be headed to the same place once we arrived: the first base bench.

"Where are you guys going?" Dave's matter of fact question was directed only to us Wasps, and as we turned to look at him, I saw that look for the first time.

The first thing you might have noticed about Dave Boettger was that he was not an imposing physical presence. The second thing you would have noticed was his shock of blond hair which, in a way, was his signature. You could easily point him out from a long distance because of it. Other than that, Dave was just an average guy in stature. You would never have known the fierce competitor he was just by looking at him.

But what he may have lacked in physical presence he more than made up for with his bearing. Bearing can be understood as creating a favorable impression in how you carry yourself, in your appearance and your personal conduct. Most good men in the world have great bearing. Another way to think of it is body language. In this case, Dave's bearing showed he meant business;

with his head tilted forward slightly and his hands at his hips you could see he was completely focused on the task at hand. He was ready for battle. This might just be coach pitch baseball to a bunch of young boys with few baseball skills, but his bearing left no doubt that he took it very seriously.

At that time of the day, the stand of trees separating our field from the rifle range cast just enough of a shadow to cover the first base bench, putting it in the shade and making it much cooler. The third base bench, on the other hand, was in the full sun. Replying to Dave's question, my teammate Billy pointed to the first base bench and said, "we're gonna go sit on this bench, it's in the shade."

Dave's expression remained laser focused as he said, "No, we always sit over here," pointing to the roasting hot third base bench.

Minor grumbling ensued from a couple of Wasps as we moved to the third base bench.

"Take a seat," said Dave.

I didn't say a word as the beads of sweat had started to stream down my face. Dave stood in front of the bench and waited until we had all turned our focus to him. Finally, he looked at us and said something I'll never forget.

"Do you know why we always sit here?" he asked.

I'm sure we were all wondering that very thing when he answered his own question, "because we're tougher than they are," he said, gesturing towards the Bees who were sitting in the relative comfort of the first base bench. "Let them sit in the shade. Sitting in the shade makes you soft and we're not soft. All right?"

We all kind of nodded even if some thought Dave was off his rocker. What struck me about this brief exchange was how

Dave delivered his message. It was so matter of fact, with almost no emotion, but heavy on conviction. He wasn't angry or condescending in his tone. No, his remarks were clearly meant to teach us our first important lesson: to be a winner, you must be mentally tough, you must be able to overcome your circumstances. You must learn to become resilient. Success in this world doesn't come easily, and you will never be a winner if you choose to take the easy road. The Wasps, we learned that very first day, would never take the easy road.

Indirectly, Dave's message was one I'd already heard and witnessed thanks to my dad and brothers. Dad would sometimes regale us with stories of the great Howdy Myers, his beloved high school football coach. Dad would recount with a certain degree of joy how tough the pre-season camps were and how demanding Coach Myers had been. But the results were conference championships. I'd seen how Jimmy and Fred would work out during the heat of summer of Virginia Beach in preparation for their own football seasons. They both were always starters on their respective teams. And I'd seen Mike Keville and all the other lifeguards bust their butts every week during the grueling drill. But this was the first time the message had been directed at me and it was music to my ears! I was so ready for it and in that instant, I was all in. I would take the road less traveled, the hard road, and Dave Boettger would be my guide.

The first couple of practices were somewhat of a three ringed circus. Dave and Lee Smoot put all of us Wasps and Bees through drills to assess everyone's level of ability. Since I'd "played" shortstop during the spring softball season at school, Dave put me there to start out. That decision may have been helped by the fact that I was well versed in the rules, which is important for an infielder. Nevertheless, it was clear I had a problem. I didn't know how to throw. More specifically, I didn't know how to throw with any accuracy. My friend Nicky Wilson was on first base that year and I just remember his looks of exasperation as, early on, my throws to him went everywhere around him instead of to him. But then, Dave took over.

"Look," he said to me in that same focused voice, "you're doing it all wrong. You're just using your arm and not your body."

"Oh," I replied, somewhat bewildered, "so what do I do?"

It just so happened that every weekday after baseball, around 3pm, was a block in the daily schedule called free swim. Just like it sounds, it was a time after spending the hot, dusty hour on the baseball field where everybody could go swim in the nice, cool Greenbrier River or just hang out in their tents.

So, Dave said, "Well look, if you're willing to give up free swim, we can stay here, and I can show you how to throw the right way."

"That'd be cool," I said with genuine enthusiasm, "I'm ready!"

No one had ever taken the time to work with me one-on-one before, so I jumped at the chance. For the next hour Dave Boettger sacrificed his own free time and coached me on the proper technique for throwing a baseball with accuracy.

He started by saying, "I've seen that you do pretty good on the grounders, but you're going to have to learn to move your feet to get yourself into position to make a good throw. And you'll need to start using your whole body when you throw so that your follow through will have some power and accuracy behind it."

I heard what he was saying but being a visual learner, I

had no idea what he was talking about.

Then he said, "Here, let me show you."

For the next ten minutes Dave showed me what I needed to do: first, whenever possible, be perpendicular to the target I was throwing to; second, as I began to throw, my left foot needed to stride toward the target; and three, I needed to push off with my back right foot and follow through with my throw so that my throwing hand was pointing to the target after I released the ball.

"I think I got it," I said.

"All right," said Dave, "Let's try a couple."

Dave stood at first base, and I was at my position at short-stop. He'd throw me grounders and I would have to scoop them up and throw them back to him using the proper technique. We did more than just a couple. For the next 45 minutes we worked at it. It was rough going at first. It was still really hot, but Dave didn't bat an eye.

Finally, he said, "All right, I think that's enough for today. You know, if you hustle in, you still might be able to catch the last part of free swim."

That sounded good so I did hustle in but not before thanking Dave for taking his free time to help me. He shot me that laser focused look of his and said, "hey, you just keep working hard and it will come." I was hot, dirty, and sweaty but I'm not sure I can express how good I felt at that moment.

The remaining couple of weeks that first summer were uneventful. As I expected, I fell short in earning the Order of the Star; nevertheless, it was a good three weeks and looking back, I can see now how much I grew in maturity in that short amount of time. The day before the other first termers and I were to board the train and head back home, I played my last baseball game of the summer. It was yet another win for the Wasps. As we made the "hike" from the field back to the tent area, several of us Wasps walked with Dave. The conversation revolved around those of us heading home and who was coming back to camp the next summer. Dave started to talk about the Pony League "world series."

"If you guys come back next year, think about coming either for the last session or for all six weeks. That way you'll be able to take part in the world series." Dave was referring to the end of the summer series that each league played to crown a champion. It was a big deal and very competitive if for nothing more than bragging rights for a year.

"I'm pretty sure I'll be back for all six weeks," I told him.

"Great," said Dave, "I'll look forward to that. You know we're going to win it!"

That was Dave; already planting the seed for next year. But my three weeks with him had proved to me Dave knew what he was doing. In that short amount of time, his coaching had helped turn me, a boy with very average athletic ability, into something resembling a baseball player, a budding athlete. He had challenged and encouraged me and my teammates to work hard to be the best whenever we took the field; to never give up. And we learned that hard work and mental toughness does pay off because we won far more games than we lost.

On the long train ride back to Norfolk, I had ample time to think back and reflect on my first year at CG. I felt a true sense of accomplishment even if I hadn't won any awards. Just making it through the three weeks was a win for me. And I had found a true role model and mentor in Dave Boettger, someone who was willing to invest his time in me to help me reach beyond where I even imagined I could go. I couldn't wait for next summer!

The train trip to CG my second year in the summer of 1968 was totally different than the year before. I was a veteran at that point and, to a certain extent, knew what to expect. This time I was ready for the sunset, the length of the trip, and felt much more confident about what lay ahead. I had devised a plan of attack to help me secure an Order of the Star by summer's end and I was excited about my second season as a Wasp. Dave had been moved to Director of Activities which kept him very busy. Nevertheless, baseball was on his mind.

"Hey, welcome back!" he said when he first saw me.

"Hey Dave," I said, "it's great to be back."

"Looks like you grew some since last year," he remarked.

Dave was being nice. While many of my peers were just beginning to experience the "buds" of puberty, I was still very pre-pubescent.

"Are you ready for the season?" he asked?

"You bet," I replied, "we're gonna win it all!" I said echoing what he had said to me the previous summer.

Dave smiled and said, "you know, the Bees have a new guy this year."

Tommy Nagel hailed from Kentucky and first came to CG in 1968. He was the new guy Dave was referring to, and we all quickly learned that Tommy was a "real" baseball player. The summer before coming to CG Tommy had been on a real Little League team back home and subsequently showed up at camp with a real baseball hat and real baseball shoes. These days that's not a big deal but in 1968 you couldn't just go to the store or order those things online. The only way to get those things was to be on a real team. We were in awe.

The CG baseball "commissioners" made two very important decisions upon Tommy's arrival at camp. First, Tommy would play in the Pony League even though he had played in Little League back home. He might have been able to physically compete up with the Minor League guys, but Tommy was not a big kid; in fact he was a bit short. So, they decided he would do better at the Pony level. Plus, the Bees needed help as the Wasps had won the world series the previous summer and returned a loaded roster.

The second decision was that Tommy would not be allowed to wear his baseball shoes for games. The rest of us were all relieved to hear that because for some odd reason we felt the shoes gave him an unfair advantage. It was enough that they did let him wear his hat!

As things got rolling at camp it became clear that Tommy was, in fact, a good baseball player and a good guy as well. He was very confident and everyone knew it, but he never crossed the line of being cocky about it. He had a soft Kentucky drawl that was unknowingly endearing and carried himself as though he could handle anything. It was clear that the Pony League of 1968 was going be highly competitive, just the way Dave liked it.

I continued to thrive under Dave's coaching and mentorship. Just as he had done the previous year, he took his own time during free swim one day to help me with another challenge: fly balls. It seemed the more I was willing to work at getting better, the more Dave was willing to help. Things really started to click for me on the baseball field and my competitive spirit started to soar, all a byproduct of Dave's tutelage. But a lot of it was also due to Tommy Nagel. He and I came to be seen as the best players on our respective teams and neither of us wanted to lose even one game. The Pony League in 1968 did turn out to be highly competitive and by the time the world series came around at the end of the summer, it was a toss-up as to whether the Wasps or the Bees would be champ. The series came down to the final game.

"What will you do if the ball is hit to you?"

I'd heard Dave ask us that question for what seemed like a thousand times before, and it was only later I realized he was yet again teaching us another valuable life lesson: always be prepared for anything. In the game of baseball, especially as an infielder, you must make split-second decisions about what to do depending on where the ball is hit. If you think about what you need to do <u>after</u> the ball is hit, the odds are you won't do the right thing. Consequently, thinking about all the things you might do <u>before</u> the ball is hit will greatly increase your chances of doing the right thing. It was a discipline I embraced, which helped me become a pretty good shortstop.

It's also the reason the Wasps took the final game, by one run, to win the Pony League world series in 1968. At a pivotal time late in the game, we had men on base with a tied score. After a hit to the infield, one unfortunate Bee infielder, for a split second, hesitated in deciding where to go with the ball and that was all it took. One Wasp run scored, and we held on to win the game.

I had never won anything in my life and the elation I felt as we stormed the field was exhilarating. I was on top of the world. All the work I had put in, with Dave's help and encouragement had paid off. As I looked over at him, he just had a wry smile along with a tremendously satisfied look on his face. Tommy, clearly the most talented player in the league, along with all his Bee teammates, was understandably disappointed. But the talk

quickly turned to how "epic" a year it had been for the Pony
League and how cool it was that it came down to the wire. Win,
lose or draw, most males just relish being in the game, being in
the arena and competing. I think we all knew it had been a special
experience. And then the conversation turned to the upcoming
awards ceremony and who was coming back to camp the next
summer.

On the day of the year end awards ceremony, camp was
abuzz with conversation and activity. Everyone was packing up
as we were all to leave camp the next day to return home. The
awards ceremony was a big deal because, frankly, not everybody
got awards back then. It was still a time where you actually had to
earn them. They truly meant something. Individually, I already
knew I had earned the coveted Order of the Star by a slim one
point, and I knew I would be getting some patches that I had
earned on the archery range, but that was it. And, I hadn't given
a lot of thought about the following summer; things at home were
a little uncertain and I was just looking forward to getting back
to Virginia Beach.

That afternoon, as we were in our tent packing up, someone asked me directly if I planned on returning to camp the next
year.

"Yeah, probably," I said rather hesitantly.

But then I added, "but if I win a trophy, I might not."

To this day I'm not sure why I added the last part about
a trophy. Very few trophies were awarded and then only to the
best camper in an activity. I was a long shot, at best, in any of the
activities I participated in.

Not long after that conversation, Dave happened to walk
by my tent and stopped when he saw me. "Hey," he said, "looking

forward to the awards ceremony? You know we're (meaning the Wasps) going to be getting our ribbons (yes, just ribbons) for winning the world series."

"Can't wait, "I said.

"All right, see you later," he replied and then walked on.

After an early dinner, we all made our way to the Hall for the awards ceremony, the last official event of the summer. The Hall had a raised stage that spanned the width of one end of the building and as we walked in, I could see a long table on the stage with trophies and the other awards to be handed out. Also seated on stage were the activity heads as well as other senior staffers. Dave, being the Head of Activities that year, oversaw the ceremony and as things got rolling, I felt a degree of sadness; it had been a great summer and a part of me was sorry it was coming to an end.

As expected, I got my archery patches and received my Order of the Star. I felt a great sense of pride and accomplishment as the Wasps were called up on stage to receive their ribbons. The ribbons were handed to us by Mr. Stobbs, the activity head for baseball. Mr. Stobbs was an older gentleman and a friend of the owners of camp. He had been a real baseball man in his younger days and his position at camp was largely ceremonial as he delegated his daily duties to younger counselors.

When the time came to hand out the coveted trophies for the most valuable camper in each activity, Mr. Stobbs stepped up to announce and present for the three baseball leagues. The Pony League was last and as Mr. Stobbs looked at the card with the winner's name, we all waited to hear him call Tommy Nagel's name. It was a no brainer. "This year's most valuable player in the Pony League is...Shep Jordan?" he announced, somewhat puzzled. For a split second, you could hear a pin drop. And then the crowd started to buzz. I was stunned; wasn't sure what to do.

The guy next to me elbowed me and said, "Hey man, that's you! Go get your trophy." I slid out of my seat and made my way to the stage to receive my trophy. All I could think was, isn't this supposed to go to Tommy? Mr. Stobbs hadn't a clue who I was and as I shook his hand and received my trophy I glanced over at Dave. He was wearing that same wry, satisfied smile on his face that I had seen when we won the final game of the world series.

When it was all over, we left the Hall to head back to the tent area. I was still in a minor state of shock as well wishers came up to congratulate me. To his immense credit, Tommy came over and said, "Hey man, good job, I'll see you next summer," unofficially laying down the gauntlet for the following summer.

I finally caught up with Dave. "How about you!" he said with as big a grin as I had ever seen on him.

"But Dave," I started.

"No!" he interrupted as his expression instantly returned to that same no nonsense look I had grown accustomed to. He knew what I was about to say.

"No!" he reiterated, "You earned this!"

"But Dave, Tommy's a better player than me," I argued.

"Maybe," he replied, "but nobody worked harder than you, nobody wanted it more than you, and nobody helped his teammates play better than you. You deserve this award. I'm very proud of you."

As good as I felt, part of me still wasn't convinced, and Dave could see that. I had learned a lot from Dave Boettger over two summers but what he said to me next, I will carry forever.

"Listen," he said, putting his hand on my shoulder,

looking me square in the eye, "never forget, you don't have to be the most talented to be the most valuable. You proved that this year."

That was a concept my 11-year-old mind had never considered, but in that instant it all made sense. The next morning, we all boarded the train to head back home. I never saw Dave Boettger or Camp Greenbrier again.

I knew before leaving camp that summer that I might not be back again. The reason was purely financial as my dad had gotten himself into a bind in the real estate market earlier that year. He had purchased a second house with the intent of flipping it. We already lived in a nice house in a great part of town, within bike riding range of my friends and the beach.

Turns out, Dad was initially unable to sell the additional house at a price he was hoping for. I'm not sure how long he paid for two mortgages but, at some point, it got to be too much of a burden financially. Enough of a burden that we ended up selling our own house and moving to an apartment complex in another part of town. Dad eventually did sell the second house, probably at a loss, but as they say, the die had been cast. From that point on frugality was the name of the game and going away to camp was one of the victims.

Unlike Mike Keville, whom I lost track of over the years, I did think about Dave periodically. It helped I had a trophy to look at to remind me of him. Every now and then I would wonder what had made Dave the kind of unique person he was; what made him tick. As easy going and affable as he was generally, when there was a mission to accomplish or competition to be waged, he transformed into a completely different person.

By all accounts Dave had a strong drive to be the best,

almost like he needed to constantly prove himself somehow. And that attitude permeated all the way down to his players in the Pony League. But here's the thing: Dave never held his Major League teammates or the players he coached more accountable than he did himself. I'll never forget the time he came up to bat during the Major League world series my second summer. With that same focused, determined look we all knew, Dave stepped into the batter's box and promptly proceeded to strike out. After the third strike, he calmly walked back to the bench even though his body language screamed how angry he was with himself. Nobody on his team said a word to him; they knew better. And as he walked to a spot on the end of the bench to sit down, several of his teammates moved to give him a little space. Everyone knew it was best to leave Dave alone at times like this and let him deal with it in his own way. I watched him intently as he just stared at the ground in front of him, clearly processing his momentary failure. But once the inning was over and his team returned to the field, he had moved on. What was it with this guy?

It was only after digging into Dave's past that I was able to put some of the pieces of this man's complicated life puzzle together. What I learned is that he and I shared similar experiences, which helped me to understand the man I had admired so much and who taught me timeless life lessons.

Dave was born and raised in a middle-class family of German descent in Cincinnati Ohio. His parents were seven years apart in age and were married in 1929. Like me, Dave was the youngest in his family which included, like me, two older brothers. And like me, he was an unexpected, late addition to his family. Unlike me though, Dave's arrival in the world came significantly later than his siblings. At the time of his birth in

1945, Dave's father was 48 years old and his mother 41, typically a time when many people of that era were just becoming grandparents. His brothers were 16 and 13 years older, respectively. Essentially, Dave was an only child growing up in a home with much older parents who likely hadn't planned to be parenting a child so young during their midlife.

My sense, having also grown up in a home with a mom of German descent, is that Dave learned early on that life isn't always fair, so you'd better just face that fact and learn to deal with it. Nothing is ever sugar coated in a home like that so nurturing generally takes a back seat to learning to deal with reality. You can either steel yourself to overcome life's challenges or you can let them defeat you.

I can only speculate that it must have been tough for Dave growing up. I'm certain his ever-present drive to succeed was fostered as a youngster who, like me, was desperate for validation and a feeling that he belonged. One way to accomplish that is by succeeding in overcoming challenges. So, it's not surprising then that Dave understood about mental toughness; he lived it.

Like three of my other heroes, Dave became a high school teacher and coach. He spent his professional life serving youth and being a role model for countless students. But it turns out that his life after CG did not read like a happy ending.

His last summer at CG was 1978. Dave never married and the story is that he fell head over heels for a woman who felt the same about him. Unfortunately, she was already married. Unlucky in love, he apparently never recovered. And as the single brother among his two siblings, he ended up living at home and taking care of his aged parents for a number of years-always the dutiful son, stoically taking on life's challenges. Dave had always been a heavy smoker and on March 20, 2009, cancer took him. He died in a hospice facility; he'd just turned 64 years old.

In John, chapter 16 verse 33 of the Bible, Jesus proclaims, "in this world you will have trouble." Man, he wasn't kidding! And you don't even have to be a Christian to know he's right. Trouble is lurking around every corner. So why is it, especially during the last 30 years, we as a culture seem to be doing everything possible to shield young people from this reality? Why aren't we challenging kids to embrace the trouble this world will throw at them and then teach them how to overcome it?

I believe that deep down, the soul of a male needs and secretly desires this kind of challenge. We need dragons to slay, mountains to climb, rivers to cross and the Pony League world series to win. It's how God made us; we're not intended to take it easy or to take the easy path. No, we are intended to be strong so that we are always able to face head-on the trouble this world will throw at us. Dave Boettger understood and modeled this truth and I feel blessed to have been able to learn from him.

So, what might Dave's example mean to you as a role model and mentor? The first piece of wisdom to glean from Dave's example is understanding that adversity, such as always sitting in the hot 3rd base sun and missing free swims to practice and get better, is truly the foundation for success. Instill in those you lead and mentor that nothing of any real value comes easily in life, and the things that end up meaning the most to you are the things you had to work hardest for.

Encourage them to embrace that mental toughness, resilience and perseverance are essential in life and that each can be cultivated and made stronger. Push those who look to you for direction to reach far beyond the place they thought they could go but always be there to pick them back up if/when they fall short.

And take heart; unfortunately, in today's world, not all will respond positively to the example set by Dave Boettger and that's just life. But then, just think about that one young man whom you <u>do</u> reach, the one whose name will be called when he least expects it, in large part because you were a positive influence in his life.

Dave Boettger

4

Jett Colonna

"As iron sharpens iron, so one person sharpens another"
Proverbs 27:17

"Courage is being scared to death and saddling up anyway"
John Wayne

"Flea flick right, on two," our quarterback, Sam McGann said in a low tone. "Flea flick right, on two," he repeated as we clapped our hands and broke the huddle.

I was a 7th grader and a running back on my 6th/7th grade intramural football team at Norfolk Academy in the fall of 1970. The "flea flick" was my play. It seemed to work every time we ran it.

Once we were lined up, Sam began the cadence, "Down... set, hup... hup!" On the second "hup" the center snapped the ball to Sam. I was lined up about two yards behind him and to his right. I began moving toward the line of scrimmage, giving the impression that Sam would be handing the ball off to me. But it was a fake and after feigning the handoff to me, Sam dropped back to pass. My job was to then find my way quickly around the right end, so that I had a clear path up the right sideline.

Meanwhile, Sam threw his usual perfect spiral to the right end, Richard Bowers who had run a 10-yard hook pattern. After Richard caught the ball (and he always did!) defenders naturally converged on him, paying no attention to the fact I was 5 yards behind and running up field. Just before being tackled, Richard lateralled the ball to me, and I sprinted untouched, to the end zone for a score.

For every football team at any level that's ever run this play, its known as the hook and lateral, not the flea flick. But, like my days as a Wasp under Dave Boettger at Camp Greenbrier, we weren't like every other team. That's because our coach was Jett Colonna, who, like Dave Boettger, was not like all the other coaches. He, too, had a specific way he liked to do things. Coach Colonna had just started his second year as a Lower School teacher/coach at Norfolk Academy, having first arrived on campus the previous fall of 1969. For me, he came along just at the right time.

In looking back before that, my triumphant return from Camp Greenbrier in the summer of 1968, Pony League MVP trophy in hand, was the last good feeling I would have for a while. I'm certain one underlying reason was our family having to move from a great neighborhood to an apartment complex earlier that year. Gone was a front and back yard to play in and woods across the street to explore; things I think all adventurous young boys need. Instead, I had row upon row of apartments and lots of asphalt. I was somewhat embarrassed by our economic fall from grace, and I ended up carrying that emotion into the school year. In the fall of 1968, a year before Jett Colonna came to NA, I began my 6th grade year which would bring other changes that I would not adapt to very well.

In those days, the Lower School at Norfolk Academy consisted of grades 1 through 7. For grades 1 through 5, there was just one teacher in the classroom, always a female, who taught all the subjects. But, starting with 6th grade, instead of having just one teacher for all subjects, there would be several different teachers for different subjects. So, for the first time, I would have a male teacher, and not just one as it turned out, but two.

On the surface that might seem inconsequential unless you consider that most students spend a large chunk of their day at school. Teachers and coaches are technically considered "in loco parentis," literally meaning, in place of the parent. It's clear that the role of teachers and coaches is of significant importance in the development of the students in their charge. That's especially true for boys on the cusp of puberty, like 6th graders, who are at a critical point in life and needing good male role models and mentors.

But there was another wrinkle added to the start of my 6th grade year: girls. Girls were already a part of the 8th-12th grade student body, but in the fall of 1968, girls were added to the Lower School ranks. Although classes were segregated by gender, free time like recesses and lunch were not and there was plenty of intermingling during those times. But I wasn't yet ready for intermingling with girls, and this just added to the social pressures I was already feeling. Maybe having male teachers as good role models might help me somehow?

My math teacher that year was a gentleman named Mr. Gibb, who was new to the school. I can say with confidence, having become a teacher myself, that teaching did not come naturally to him. Back then, all I knew was that he was a difficult guy to warm up to. He seemed to always be wearing a scowl on his face which gave the appearance that he smelled something bad. Math was my weakest subject and Mr. Gibb had little patience if you did not pick up on things quickly enough. In retrospect, I realize he just didn't have the ability to connect to our age group and felt uncomfortable in the classroom. He left after that one year, but I'll never forget the final parent conference at the end of the school year when things were unravelling for me. Mr. Cumiskey, the Lower School head, had me attend the meeting, along with my mom, so I could hear what the teachers had to say.

When it was Mr. Gibb's turn to provide insight, he had the audacity to look at my mother and say to her with me sitting right there, "After a year like this, I don't see any way that Shep can pass the final exam."

He said it with a degree of contempt that suggested he was offended in some way that I couldn't do better in his class. I had the last laugh though; I got a D on the final and actually passed his class for the year. An inconsequential victory perhaps, but nevertheless, I wasn't concerned with impressing Mr. Gibb.

Also starting his first year at NA that year was my science teacher, Mr. Varner. A Texas native, Mr. Varner was generally a good guy and very likeable. He had a Texas drawl and talked and moved at a slower pace than Mr. Gibb who frequently seemed to have consumed way too much caffeine. A recent graduate of the University of Virginia, Mr. Varner spent just two years at NA, doing what I would describe as "playing out the clock" by teaching while he figured out what he really wanted to do with his life. Although I wouldn't say Mr. Varner wasn't a good role model, I would say that the classroom and teaching were just not his calling.

As I previously explained, my meeting with Charlie Cumiskey at the end of that 1968-1969 school year changed the track of my life: I would be required to repeat 6th grade the following year. All these years later, I can look back and see that what I needed in a male role model at that time was simply more than Mr. Varner or Mr. Gibb were able to provide. What I needed was to feel a sense of stability and compassion from a male teacher I could admire, someone who was clearly committed to the school and to the students as well. I needed a real mentor. Fortunately for me, that person was about to show up in my life.

When I saw Jett Colonna that first day of school in the fall of 1969, I knew right away he was different from the other male teachers I'd had. In many ways he reminded me of Mike Keville, lean and tan with brown hair made sandy blond by the sun, I learned early on that among his passions were surfing and staying physically fit, long before that became a mainstream thing to do. He would have gotten along well with the lifeguards of the Virginia Beach Patrol!

But there was something else about him. In the Marine Corps we called it having command presence and Jett had a large dose. You could tell just by looking at him that he was in charge. He moved with a sense of purpose but always at a measured pace, almost as if he were gliding. His facial expressions typically mirrored the way he moved, purposeful and intentional.

Many years later, former student, Sarah Goodson, NA Class of 1999, eloquently described her first impression of Jett, "Mr. Colonna had a very square jaw and intense eyes that felt like they were sizing you up for a fight, not that I planned on squaring up to the guy, but he had an air about him that if I was thinking about throwing a punch, he would win."

She was right. He didn't have to say a word, yet we all knew there were boundaries with Mr. Colonna and God help the few misguided souls that might ever challenge those boundaries! The truth is, in subtle ways, he _was_ sizing you up but not in some dark, confrontational way. Authenticity, or perhaps more accurately, integrity, meant everything to him. He could detect BS from a mile away and he would call you out in an instant and expose your fakeness.

He would say things like, "Son, do you and I need to go have a private conversation or are you gonna change your attitude right this minute?" He rarely raised his voice at times like these because it wasn't necessary. His tone was sharp and straight to the point. Anytime Mr. Colonna started by addressing you as "son" you knew you were about to be "reminded", in a way that would be very uncomfortable, of your proper place in the world.

The bottom line is, with Jett Colonna you simply were never permitted to hide behind false words and bravado. Doing so would be an obvious sign of weakness. Jett knew and lived the reality that men need to be strong not just physically and mentally, but in their souls as well. What a valuable and important life lesson for every male.

Over time, though, we also saw there was another, dare I say it, softer side to Mr. Colonna that balanced his tough side. As Sarah Goodson puts it, "He had a magical way of finding the connections between all of the students to make everyone feel comfortable in the group." She was right again and because of these attributes, I liked him right away. I wondered at the time if he would be the kind of role model I was unconsciously yearning for?

Jett taught Social Studies, geography for 6th grade and Ancient Civilizations for 7th grade, which meant I had him as a classroom teacher for two years. Unlike math, these were subjects I loved and where I enjoyed success. I felt confident that I would thrive with Mr. Colonna. On that first day of my second attempt at 6th grade, he won me over simply by knowing my name.

"Good morning boys, my name is Mr. Colonna, "he said as he wrote his name on the board. I was a little on edge since I was beginning the new school year with new classmates. Plus, I wondered if Mr. Colonna knew I was repeating 6th grade; would he think less of me as a result? He sat down at the desk at the front of the room and pulled out his gradebook.

"OK," he said, "let's go over the roll. Raise your hand when I call your name."

Oh God, I thought, here we go again. As he began to work his way alphabetically through the list of students, "Batten, Brundage, Dickinson," I knew when he came to my name, I'd have to correct him and then provide an explanation. You see, my family doesn't pronounce my last name like most of the rest of the world does. And that's because we're very stubborn. Since the year 1610, my line of the Jordans has steadfastly stuck to the old Elizabethan era pronunciation which sounds like Jerdan. Over the years, many of our name simply got tired of having to explain this phenomenon and just went with the conventional pronunciation instead. But not us Jordans!

He continued, "Hill, Irvin, Jones."

Oh God, I'm next!

"Jordan," he called out.

Wait, what?

When he got to my name, Mr. Colonna pronounced it correctly and flawlessly, like he'd known me for a long time. I was in a minor state of shock, but then I realized he was looking at me, so I quickly remembered to raise my hand. But here's the thing: in looking at me, I saw no sign of judgment from him because I was repeating 6th grade; no quizzical look questioning the pronunciation of my name. You know those looks when you see them. No, his expression clearly reflected his recognition of who I was and that he was good with it all. In a Mike Keville kind of way, Jett Colonna, simply by knowing and making sure to pronounce my name correctly, showed me that I mattered to him.

It was a small but nevertheless meaningful show of respect, the one thing young males crave the most. The stress I had just been feeling melted away. I knew right then that Jett Colonna would be someone I looked up to; someone whose example I would try to follow.

I looked forward to Mr. Colonna's class every day for the two years I had him. Not only did I love the subject matter, but he also had a way of captivating a classroom. It turned out that he was an adept storyteller. One day that first year he decided that since it was Halloween, he would start class by telling us a scary Halloween story. He turned out the lights in the classroom and pulled the shades to make the room darker. I don't remember the story but I do remember how easily he drew us all in as he skillfully proceeded with the story. He started out sitting behind his desk at the front of the room but about halfway through the story he slowly got up and began moving methodically from one side of the room to the other. We were hypnotized, hanging on every word! Just as he got to the climactic point in the story, he suddenly threw his arms out at us and let out a shockingly loud "AAAHHHHH!" Scared us half to death! He got this grin on his face which revealed to us that underneath that tough exterior was a pretty cool guy.

Most of his stories though, were meant to teach us life lessons, although we never realized that's what they were. We just loved hearing his stories and not having to do classwork for a few minutes! Usually, the stories centered around how to treat people the right way but also, as males, the necessity of being strong and tough in this world.

One morning that first year he decided to share with us a story about a meal his wife had recently made. Having recently been married to his wife Lea, he told us that she had worked very hard to prepare a special meal for him.

"Boys," he started with a grimace on his face, "my wife's a pretty good cook but when I took that first bite, well, it was awful."

The classroom responded, "Oooohhhh nooo!"

"Yeah," he said, "pretty bad."

"What did you do?" we asked, on the edge of our seats.

"Well," he responded, "of course she asked me how it tasted."

"What did you say?" we implored.

He said, "Well, I told her it was perfect and how much I appreciated the effort she had made in making it special."

We couldn't believe it, "No waaaay, really?"

But then he gave us the moral of the story, "Listen boys, when someone goes out of their way to do something for you, especially your wife, you better show your appreciation, no matter what. I finished the meal because it was the right thing to do to show my appreciation."

That message: always do the right thing, no matter how tough, was one I'd heard consistently at home and one I would continue to hear, not just from Mr. Colonna, but from all the men I admired.

Then, one day the following year in 7th grade, he captivated us with this story, "Boys, I'll never forget the day we played the Norview Pilots," he started.

Mr. Colonna was born and raised in Norfolk and attended Matthew Fontaine Maury High School. Known simply as Maury, the school is the oldest public school in Norfolk, opening in 1910. Norview High School followed in 1922 and Granby High School in 1939. In the relatively small city of Norfolk, you might correctly assume the rivalries between these schools were (and still are) quite intense. Jett was a captain of the Maury Commodore football team his senior year in the fall of 1960. This story, we learned, would be about toughness. And he would use football, something we were all familiar with, as the example.

"It was a bitter slugfest," he continued, "back and forth we went. Bragging rights were on the line." At this point in the story, Mr. Colonna was standing at the front of the classroom and he became very animated in his movements, as though he were back on the playing field. We loved it. His facial expression took on a rigid tenseness and his eyes became laser focused as if he were staring down the enemy; this was his "game face" and we knew the story was about to get intense.

"Towards the end of the game, Norview was driving the ball downfield on us. We had the lead but we needed to stop them."

Jett was a linebacker on defense. He continued, "we [the defense] were tired yet determined. It got to be 4th down and one on our 30-yard line and they needed to score a touchdown to take the lead. Time was running out. So, they decided they had to go for it. They broke the huddle and came to the line of scrimmage."

Then Mr. Colonna moved to his right as though he were taking up his position on the field, ready to mount a defense once again.

"When they snapped the ball, a hole opened in the line of scrimmage almost immediately on my side of the field. I quickly went to fill the hole."

He then took two quick steps forward as though he were actually filling the hole.

He continued, "I saw that the running back had been given the ball. He was coming straight at me. At that point, I knew it was just him and me. So, I broke down into my football stance (feet shoulder width apart, knees bent, butt down, back straight, head up and arms out)."

He proceeded to actually get into a football stance and with a fire in his eyes it looked like he could suit up and play again.

"I knew it would be painful, "he said, "but I stood my ground and met the ball carrier in the hole. BOOM!"

He came out of his stance and clapped his hands.

"Boys, I've never been hit so hard in my life, actually saw stars, but the running back went down, short of the first down!"

The classroom erupted with applause along with a few ooohs and aahhs.

And then, as always, came the moral; we were all on the edge of our seats, "You know boys, whether its football or just life in general, there's going to be times where you have to 'fill the hole.' You know it's likely to be painful but you still have to do it. You can't back down."

I soaked it all up.

Although Coach Colonna coached JV football and JV basketball in his early years at NA, the only time he coached me directly was intramural football my 7th grade year. Like Dave Boettger, his reputation for toughness, for "filling the hole" and always doing the right thing were already well known. So, when I learned he would be coaching my football team, I was both elated and a little hesitant at the same time. I knew he would give his heart and soul to coaching our team but I also knew my degree of toughness would be tested by him daily.

For instance, one of Coach's favorite drills was called "bull in the ring," and if you've ever witnessed a bullfight, you know the bull ring is round and the bull is let out into the ring to face the matador. Likewise, for his drill, roughly 10 to 12 players would form a ring about 10-15 yards in diameter. Coach would choose one player to be the "bull" and that player would take his place in the center of the ring. Coach, who was also in the ring, would then take a football and randomly throw the ball to one of the players making up the ring. Once that player caught the ball, his task was to then run at the bull in the center of the ring. The bull's job was to tackle the ball carrier.

There was absolutely no place to hide in this drill, and that was the basic point. There was no avoiding a collision in the center of the ring but if you, as Coach called it, "go half speed", he'd make you do it again until he was satisfied you were going "full speed." Once Coach felt the bull had done enough, he'd call another player from the ring to take the bull's place in the center of the ring.

Coach Colonna had another toughness drill that he used at the Junior Varsity level. I don't think it had a name but I'll just call it the 2x4 drill. You knew the drill would be part of that day's practice when you saw Coach walking out to the practice field with a piece of 2x4 lumber on his shoulder. He looked like a gladiator walking out to the arena in preparation for some great battle. Picture it as a reverse tug-of-war.

Coach would plunk the hunk of wood (probably 8' in length) on to the ground and bark out, "alright boys, two lines, let's go!" Players would then form two lines, one at each end of the 2x4.

"First man up!," he'd yell and with that the first two

players in each line would get down in a three-point stance at their end of the 2x4.

"Here we go…ready," and then Coach would blow his whistle to start.

As a player, you understood the intent of this drill was to meet the other player head on and do whatever it took to move him back to his end of the 2x4. Conversely, he would try to do the same to you. When Coach blew his whistle to begin each group, you just knew there was no place to hide; no going half speed. The hunk of 2x4 served not only as a prop but also as a guide. Each grouping had to stay over the 2x4; if you or your opponent happened to veer to one side of it or the other, Coach would blow his whistle and make you start over. There was no easy way out. Typically, each grouping would end in a stalemate but never before Coach would allow the battle to go on for what seemed like forever.

Now, to those not familiar with football it might seem as though these drills were just a bit barbaric and mindless. That's fair but looking back, I can't think of one time where anyone ever got hurt during these drills although I did get crushed once by my friend Wes Graves during a bull in the ring session.

But, as much as the players dreaded these drills, when they were over, somehow, we felt stronger and more confident. We felt tougher, like iron sharpening iron.

I hope at this point in the narrative you are picking up on some common threads among my heroes: anything worth achieving in this life will require hard work; there's no easy way, no shortcuts. Hard work and having the courage to step up to any challenge will not only make you stronger it'll make you a better person overall.

I want to share one more important Coach Colonna 7th grade intramural football story. It started with a play (not the flea flick) where our quarterback, Sam, pitched me the ball and I began to sweep around the right side of the line of scrimmage. When I got close to the sideline, I planted my right foot to turn up field. Just then, out of nowhere it seemed, my friend Ross Jaffe, playing on defense for the other team, crashed into my left side, right at the thigh level. Until that moment, I'd never experienced what is commonly referred to as a "charley horse." I tried to pop back up after the tackle but immediately fell back to the ground in a heap as the pain signal made its way to my brain. It was pain I'd never felt before and if you've ever had a charley horse you know what I mean. It initially feels much worse than it really is. Guys from both teams quickly gathered around to make sure I was OK, with the secondary, unconscious intent of seeing how well (or not) I was handling the pain. It's like when you slow down at a car accident to see how bad it is. Coach Colonna was on the other side of the field and I could see he was making his way, as always with purpose and at a measured pace, over to where I lay.

"What's wrong?" he asked matter of factly in a calm tone that suggested he wasn't overly concerned.

"It's my leg," I replied, trying to make it seem as if it were nothing even though it hurt like hell.

Coach knelt down and said, "Show me where it hurts." So, I pointed to the spot on the side of my left leg, just about at mid-thigh.

"Does your knee hurt at all," he asked.

"No sir," I replied trying to appear calm, "just my thigh."

He pondered for a second and offered his diagnosis, "Looks like Jaffe gave you nice charley horse. Can you get up now?" The initial shock and pain had indeed subsided but my leg was still very sore and tight. I got up.

Coach then said to me, "It's almost halftime so go over to the sideline and try and walk it off."

I limped over to the sideline and I kept moving during the 5-minute halftime while Coach talked to the team about our first half efforts. Then, just as halftime was ending, he looked over at me and said, "Jordan…you going to be able to go the second half?" The rest of our team, all of whom had taken a knee while Coach was talking, turned, and looked up at me. I hesitated for a split second because if we're completely honest with ourselves, we <u>all</u> have that little voice inside that at times like these tries to convince us its ok to take the easy way out. "Heck," it says to us, "you just got really dinged, no one expects you to continue. It's no problem to call it a day. Everyone will understand." You know the voice I'm talking about.

But this was clearly a "filling the hole" moment for me, and at once I knew it. Coach wasn't pressuring me one way or the other, no; he made it clear the choice to continue to play, albeit a little banged up, or to take the easy way and call it a day was mine and mine alone. I knew there was only one answer so I said, "I'm good Coach."

My dad would occasionally say, "You know, sometimes you just have to play hurt."

It was a football metaphor he liked to use to describe any situation where you might not be 100% but you nevertheless still need to get the job done. People are depending on you.

While it may seem like 7th grade intramural football is not all that important, in a relative sense, when you're a boy in 7th grade, its huge. As a running back on the team, my role was fairly important and a large part of me didn't want to let my teammates down by not playing the second half. More importantly though, a much larger part of me didn't want to let Coach Colonna down. I did not for one second want him to think I didn't measure up, that I didn't have what it takes. That's the kind of inspiration good role models can have on young men.

The second half of the game was uneventful. My thigh remained sore but I somehow forgot about it during the heat of the battle. As the players were walking back to the locker room after the game, Coach came up and started walking with me. "How's your leg feeling?", he asked.

"It's pretty sore but I'll be ok," I responded.

"Yeah," he said, "it's probably gonna be sore for a couple of days. Be sure and put some ice on it when you get home."

"Yes sir, I will."

We continued on for several more steps and then he said, "good game today."

Those three words left an indelible mark because Coach Colonna was typically very judicious in handing out individual accolades but I knew he didn't necessarily mean I had played all that well. No, those three words were his way of confirming that, at least for that day, I had showed him and my teammates that I had what it takes, I didn't try and hide or take the easy way. I "filled the hole." It felt so good to hear that from him, and all I could think at that point was that I was just trying to follow the example he and guys like Dave Boettger and Mike Keville had already set for me.

Of course, I had no way of knowing back then that for men, life presents you with "filling the hole" moments daily. Some are bigger and more significant than others but no one escapes that reality. Looking back, I'm certain that was the lesson Coach Colonna was trying to teach us all those years ago. Every day you will have to decide, usually multiple times, do I "play hurt" or do I take the easy way?

A true, strong man will never seek the easy way.

I cannot even remotely fathom how different my life would be had I not learned and embraced this lesson from Coach Colonna......and Dave Boettger....and Mike Keville.

My 8th grade year at Norfolk Academy brought a number of changes, not the least of which was leaving the Lower School building and moving to the Middle School building on a different part of the campus. Consequently, I rarely saw Coach Colonna after that but when our paths did happen to cross, he always made a point of taking a second to see how everything was going, just as Mike Keville had done. I relished those times to re-connect with Coach, no matter how fleeting. I wish now I'd had more of those times. I graduated from Norfolk Academy in 1976 but, thankfully, I would have one more brief moment in time to be mentored by Coach Colonna.

By 1993, I'd come to a crossroads in my life. Since 1976, I had been to college, dropped out for a year and then gone back to a different college and graduated. I'd spent 7 years as an officer in the Marine Corps and about 5 years in various jobs in the corporate world. I'd been hired and I'd been fired, I'd been married, divorced, and remarried. I'd won awards and decorations and I'd been told I was no good. And, I had also been blessed with 3 boys.

As you will see in the next chapter, after my divorce in 1990 and leaving the Marine Corps, I moved back to Virginia Beach and was encouraged by another coach, Dave Trickler, to consider a career in education and coaching. That was frankly nowhere on my radar screen of potential career choices at that time.

I decided instead to enter the corporate world and became a financial consultant. For me it was all about the money at that point, the earning potential. For the next three years I worked to educate and advise clients on everything from estate planning to stock picking. In essence, I was a teacher for my clients and I was very good at helping them understand the recommendations I was making for them. But that approach never sat well with my superiors as their only concern was what was I selling that day to people who didn't really need what I was selling that day. Financial advising is a numbers game first and foremost and I eventually decided it was not the game I was destined to play.

My wife, Mary Downey, always believed that teaching and coaching were a calling for me and after much discussion with her, I decided she (and Coach Trickler) were right. I left the financial world at the end of 1993 and began 1994 unemployed, in a new house and a new baby boy but excited about the adventure that was about to unfold.

By the fall of 1994, I'd begun the process of learning exactly how to be an effective educator by enrolling in a specialized program at Old Dominion University in neighboring Norfolk. The program was designed to prepare people who've had prior military service to transition into the field of education. Early in the program's curriculum was the requirement to spend a week in a classroom somewhere, observing an experienced teacher. There was never any question who I wanted to shadow.

Although I had not seen Coach Colonna in years, I hoped to be able to spend the week in his classroom. He was still at NA, teaching Ancient Civilizations in the Middle School. So, I called

Gary Laws, the Middle School director to see if it were possible.

"You bet," said Gary, "I'll check with Jett but I'm sure there won't be a problem. It'll be great to have you back on campus."

Gary had come to NA the year after Jett so I knew him well also. A week later, I showed up to start my week of shadowing Jett Colonna.

I arrived early that Monday morning because I wanted to be there before Coach showed up. I was waiting in the Middle School front office when he walked in. Honestly, I was nervous but I'm not sure why. When he walked in, it was like I'd never been gone.

"Hey Coach!," I blurted.

He took one look at me and got a warm smile on his face, "Look at you," he said as he stuck out his hand, "you grew up!"

We shook hands, and he said, "it's good to see you. I'm excited you're getting into teaching."

"Good to see you too, Coach," I replied, "You look great."

He did look good and to my eye had hardly aged at all. He was still fit and trim and as we moved out into the hallway and began walking to his classroom, I could see he still had that commanding presence. The hallway was packed with students, many of whom greeted him as we went by. I felt as if I were with royalty as the "red sea" of students parted so as not to get in his way. I sensed initially that maybe he had mellowed to a degree. He still moved at that same measured pace and with a sense of purpose and you could still see the intensity reflected in his eyes and facial expression. He reminded me of an elder statesman, wise and seasoned in his years, who could still kick your butt if you deserved it.

"Here we are," he said as we got to his classroom.

I had forgotten how creative Coach was in setting up his classrooms. When we walked in, my jaw hit the floor. I felt as if I had transitioned back in time to the ancient civilizations that he taught. There was historical stuff everywhere but the room appeared remarkably uncluttered, as if everything were precisely where it was intended to be. It was alive. There were also random surf posters here and there, a reflection of his continued passion for surfing.

"Coach!," I said, "this is incredible!," referring to the classroom setup.

"Yeah," he replied modestly, "the kids have a lot to do with all of this."

As the students in the first class of the day began to filter into the classroom, my mind was immediately taken back to the time I was a student in Mr. Colonna's class. Everyone knew the routine: be on time, come in and take your seat and get your notebook out. As that first class started, I was reminded just how comforting it is to know what the expectations are, the boundaries not to be crossed, that those boundaries and expectations are fair and that the teacher will hold every student accountable to those standards. I was happy to see that Coach Colonna had not changed on those important things.

It was an incredible week. Coach naturally introduced me to each class that first day. True to form, he pronounced my name flawlessly and explained to the students why I was there and that I had also been a student there. He even let me "teach" a class at the end of the week.

But two things stood out for me that week. It happened to be the week of parent/teacher conferences, which took place on that Wednesday. Coach had a full slate of parents and made sure to get each parent's approval for me to observe. As I learned later at my own parent/teacher conferences, its usually the parents of the students that have no issues that show up. Those are the easy ones.

But there was one boy who was having trouble and his mom was coming in. When I say trouble, I mean he was having adolescent boy issues. For whatever reason, he was having trouble academically and socially and I noticed it the first day of class. He came in and quickly went to the seat in the back corner of the room. His facial countenance revealed an anxiousness that I recognized immediately. He proceeded to have some difficulty staying engaged in class and appeared preoccupied with other things. I seem to remember he had not completed his homework that day. This behavior continued throughout the week. Clearly, this young man just wasn't happy. I felt for him to a certain degree as I had experienced some of the same issues when I was that age.

Right before the mom came in Coach said to me, "This next one is going to be a tough one."

I didn't say a word as just then the mom walked in. Fortunately, she couldn't have been nicer. She knew full well her son was having issues and was anxious to talk to Coach about what to do. That's when I saw a side of Jett Colonna that I sensed had always been there but that he rarely let be seen (at least to students). Here was the guy who was the picture of toughness and the "filling the hole" mentality masterfully guiding a distressed mom with compassion, understanding and calmness. Despite the trouble this mom's son caused in the classroom, it was clear that Coach was nevertheless on his side. He truly wanted what was best for the boy. At that moment it hit me; Coach had a heart for the underdog.

The mom left the meeting with boundless gratitude for what turned out to be a productive meeting. "I think that went really well," I mentioned to Coach after the mom left.

"Yeah," he responded softly, "I think it did." As he spoke, I could see that he was still thinking about the meeting, going over in his mind what had been discussed. But then, "Ok," he snapped, "who's next?"

I got home that night and couldn't stop thinking about that one parent meeting and how Coach Colonna had handled it so masterfully. I wondered how someone like him could be such a proponent of physical and mental toughness and still have a deeply caring and compassionate heart. I started thinking about the things I knew would set him off like people pretending to be something they're not or taking credit for something they had no role in achieving.

After thinking about it for a bit, I saw it clearly. For Coach, it was always about the battle, the struggle, regardless of whether it was football or life. Somehow, he understood that for the underdog, the struggle was always more difficult. So, he had a heart for the ones who had to work harder to overcome the obstacles that others may not have had to endure. That was especially true if the obstacles were ones they had nothing to do with creating or obstacles that were flat out unjust. I don't know how or why, but I feel certain he must have known how that felt because it's entirely possible he'd felt the same way at some point in his life. It was almost like he was saying, "I see your challenges, I see the obstacles in front of you. I know how that feels and I'm here to motivate you to avoid taking the easy way. I'm here to help you fight the battle, overcome the struggle."

That's why, on that first day of class back in 1969, he won

me over. I was a slightly chunky, unsure kid with thick tortoise shell glasses and a weird name who was held back academically. A classic underdog and borderline loser. And yet, he knew how to pronounce my name and was never once condescending in any way. He not only taught me how to fight the battles but that I could and should fight the battles.

The other thing that stood out that week was a brief conversation Coach and I had on the way to lunch on Friday, our last day together. Sadly, it foreshadowed what I would later experience happening in the world of education. I don't know the circumstances that led to the exchange, but as Coach and I left his classroom on the way to the lunchroom, he spotted one of his male students in the classroom next to his.

"Wait just a second," he said.

I stopped and he proceeded to step into the classroom doorway to address the student, who was sitting at a desk. What followed was something I had witnessed many years prior. It started by Jett saying to the student in a stern tone, "Son…" You know the rest. Actually, I wasn't surprised that this particular student was getting a large dose of Coach's wrath over whatever he had done wrong. This kid was everything Coach disliked: a total fake. Smug and seemingly disinterested, the student sat there and listened with a look that screamed, "I don't care, you can't do anything to me. You don't matter." And then it was over but I could feel the steam coming out of Coach's ears. I didn't say a word until we got out of the building.

"What was that all about?" I asked somewhat hesitantly.

Coach just shook his head and said, "Yeah… you know."

Funny thing is, I did know. We walked a few more steps and he said, "You know Shep," all week long he'd called me

Coach; it's just a guy thing to do. In my life, he'd never called me by my first name before so I knew whatever he was going to say next was important, "I'm not sure how much longer I can keep doing this (teaching). Everything is changing. The kids don't show much respect anymore and I feel a little bit like a dinosaur. My way of doing things is dying out."

I was at a loss but said, "Coach, man, they don't know how lucky they are to have you."

He just nodded his head as we entered the lunchroom. Thankfully, Coach Colonna lasted longer than he thought he would on that Friday in 1994. He retired in 2001, 32 years after his arrival at Norfolk Academy." By that time, I was in my 5th year of teaching and coaching, using many of the techniques, both in the classroom and on the athletic fields, that I had learned from Jett.

It saddens me to say I had frankly lost track of him at that point.

If memory serves me, it was my brother Jimmy that called me about Jett. It was October 24, 2014. "Hey," he said, "did you see where Jett Colonna died?"

"What!" I replied in shock, "no way, where'd you see that?" Of course, I knew he'd seen it in the obituary section of the newspaper but I was so shocked by the news I couldn't think of anything else to say.

"It's in the obits this morning," he replied.

"He wasn't that old," I argued, "and he was always in great shape. Did it say how he died?" Jimmy replied, "Cancer. He was only 71."

"Damn it, this is not how it should have ended for him," I said. It all felt eerily similar to the feeling I had when I learned of Mike Keville's untimely death. I immediately tried to make sense of the news but, of course, I couldn't.

He's too tough to die, I thought. He was always so healthy and strong. Cancer didn't care apparently but what bothered me the most was that I hadn't even known he was sick. But that was Jett. True warrior that he was, I knew in my heart he had fought the good fight but I'm certain he wouldn't have wanted to burden anyone else with his struggle. His passing was unexpected and a shock to many who knew him.

In the weeks following his passing, the tributes flowed from all corners from those whose lives had been touched by Jett. One of the many tributes that caught my eye came from former student, Christopher O'Brien: "Mr. Colonna was one of those rare teachers who managed to bring his subject to life, engage his students (no mean feat with 14-year-olds), and most importantly, provided a friendly and sympathetic ear to them when in need. He was a great man, both in and out of the classroom, and his life touched thousands of lives. He will be missed and appreciated by all of us who had the privilege of learning from him."

There's nothing more I can add to that.

In the Old Testament book of Ecclesiastes, wise old King Solomon writes, "there's a time to every purpose under heaven." Jett had a keen sense of this. He always knew when it was time to be tough, to be a warrior, and when it was time to have compassion and empathy. This was probably his greatest lesson to me and countless others. I have many times wondered just how he seemed to be able to balance his "fierceness" with an equal measure of peace and calmness. There was a depth to his soul that I could sense but never explain.

I'm fairly certain he wasn't religious in the traditional sense, but I do believe he was deeply spiritual and found his spiritual nourishment out on the water, surfing. As a surfer myself, I can tell you there is something inexplicably spiritual and peaceful about being out on God's great ocean somewhere and riding a wave He has sent. Most surfers know this truth and it's a large part of the appeal of surfing. I think for Jett, this truth is what renewed and nourished his soul for most of his adult life. It wasn't long after learning of his passing that I ran across a copy of a poem he had penned at some point. I think it speaks volumes. Remarkably, I found it posted on the Facebook page of Jett's brother-in-law. It was written in Jett's distinctive hand:

"The last rays swept across the azure surface,
wind took its time to nestle back into the clouds,
slickness and calm came on the face of mother sea,
waves rushed forward toward their final reward on the sandy beach,
and the surfer smiled"

It's a difficult thing to get through life without having any regrets. One of mine is that I never took the opportunity to go surfing with Coach. It would have been so easy to do; I just never made the effort to reach out. What a shame. Someday though, I believe on the same beach where I hope to run into Mike Keville, I'll spot Coach Colonna, surfboard under his arm, preparing to paddle out. "Hey Jordan," he'll say, "you ready to go catch a few?"

And the surfer will smile.

Jett Colonna-1971

5

Dave Trickler

"The mentor urges us towards greatness through risk taking and threshold crossing."

From *Hinge Moments* by D. Michael Lindsay

"Failing to prepare is preparing to fail."

John Wooden, legendary UCLA basketball coach

As I've gotten older, I continually marvel at how God weaves the days of our lives in ways we don't always realize or understand until much later. Nothing in this life, I think, is random. For instance, I had no way of knowing on a cold winter day in 1965 that the guy I was watching on the basketball court would one day have a major impact on my life, as well as the lives of countless others.

"Wait till you all see this guy on our team," declared my brother Jimmy as my mom, dad, sister, and I entered the gymnasium, "he's basically unstoppable."

The team Jimmy was referring to was the Hampden-Sydney College basketball team and the "unstoppable" guy was the team's point guard. I was all of 8 years old then and hadn't a clue about the rules for basketball, but I seem to remember there were a lot of whistles from the referees, especially when this guy had the ball.

Jimmy was halfway through his freshman year at Hampden-Sydney and that weekend mom and dad dragged me and my sister to the school in Farmville, Virginia to visit and take in a basketball game. Frankly, I was a bit bored, that is until the game started and this guy began to run circles around the opposing team.

"What's his name?" I asked.

Jimmy responded, "he's Dave Trickler."

I immediately began to giggle. In my immature 8-year-old mind, "Trickler" just sounded funny to me.

In his prime, Dave Trickler stood about 5'6" tall. It would seem he had no business being on the basketball court at that height, but I soon saw for myself that he had a gift. A senior at Hampden-Sydney that year, Dave was a two-sport star in basketball and baseball. He was one of the best athletes I've ever seen.

By the fall of 1967, I had started my second year at Norfolk Academy, in the 5th grade. That same year Dave Trickler started his first year at NA as a teacher and coach, beginning a run that would span 35 years.

Before the school year started, Mom said to me, "Hey, you remember that basketball player we saw at Hampden-Sydney back when Jimmy was a freshman?"

"You mean Dave Trickler?" I said with a giggle. How could I forget a name like that? "Sure," I said, "how come?"

"Well, he's coming to school this year to teach and coach." My mom worked as a librarian at NA so she knew about things like that.

"Cool, what's he gonna coach?" I asked showing my complete, singular obsession with sports.

Mom said, "I'm pretty sure varsity basketball, varsity baseball and JV football."

In those days, football, basketball, and baseball were considered the major sports and Coach Trickler would be coaching all three, unofficially making him a pretty big deal on campus.

But it wasn't until the summer of 1969, after my first attempt at 6th grade, that I had any direct connection with Coach Trickler. That summer, instead of returning to Camp Greenbrier I began attending the daily sports camp at Norfolk Academy.

The camp was run by Royce Jones, the school's athletic director and head varsity football coach and Coach Trickler was his right-hand man. They were quite a team.

At the end of each day, the entire contingent of campers would congregate in the gymnasium to wrap things up before going home for the day. Most days Coach Jones would make some announcements or lead us all in a game of Simon Says (you wouldn't believe how difficult it was!) or maybe some songs (remember "John Jacob Jingleheimer Schmidt?"). Then, Coach Trickler would take over and he'd usually talk to us about some of the accomplishments individual campers may have had that day.

"Hey, how about that Ed, the "Flea," Kramer today," he'd say while clapping his hands. "Today he led his team to a five-point victory on the basketball court. He scored a 'career best' 10 points in the win. Where are you, Eddie?" he'd ask as he canvassed the crowd of campers. "Stand up and take a bow young man!"

It was at times like these that I first became aware that Dave Trickler had, here it comes again, command presence. But unlike Dave Boettger and Jett Colonna, Dave's bearing was less physical in nature and more subtle. He was completely comfortable in front of a large group of youngsters and seemed to relish being there. I don't know how he did it, but when he spoke to the group, it somehow felt as if he were talking directly to you. This perception usually left everyone hanging on his every word. But the one thing that made Dave Trickler stand out was his sincerity. In the 35+ years that I knew him, I never once, ever, heard him refer to himself in any conversation. Not that he didn't have many, many things to be boastful about. A star athlete in high school, Dave was the starting quarterback in football and, as an all-state point guard, he led his basketball team to the state championship in 1961. His success continued at Hampden-Sydney where he played in all 91 games of his collegiate basketball career while earning all Mason-Dixon Conference honors as a shortstop on the Tiger's baseball team. Nevertheless, he could usually be found giving others credit or just trying to find ways to provide a positive message (build others up). It was never about him and that one quality drew you to Coach Trickler; you wanted to be around him, you wanted to hear what he had to say. And once the conversation was over, you generally went away with a good feeling.

Through his focus on the achievements of others, you knew he was a man who cared about the young people in his charge. He paid attention. Some people seem to spend their time gazing in the mirror, but Dave Trickler looked out the window at the world beyond.

I'll always remember one day that summer, when Coach happened to see me shooting baskets in the gym. Even though I was just a 6th grader, I already felt as if my hope of ever being good enough to one day be on our varsity school team was slim. Nevertheless, I liked basketball and played pick-up games with friends all the time.

I'm not sure he even knew my name at that point but he wandered over to me and said, "Hey, can I show you something that will help your shot?"

This would turn out to be my very first one-on-one interaction with Coach Trickler. There would be many more in the future. At the time, I thought to myself, "Are you kidding, you're the Varsity coach and you want to help me, a dorky little 6th grader, get better?" His offer caught me a little off-guard, so all I could mutter was, "Sure Coach."

He held out his hands and said, "Ok, let me see the ball." As I passed him the ball he continued, "If you just improve a couple of things with your shooting form, it will make a huge difference for you."

"The first thing," he began, "is that your shots are too flat. You need to put more of an arc on your shot."

With that, he proceeded to show me what he meant by lofting a shot from about 15 feet that had plenty of arc and was nothing but net going through the basket.

"Kinda like that," he said, "see what I mean?"

I did see it, and I nodded my head, but he wasn't finished. I quickly learned that, for Coach Trickler, simply knowing what to do was never good enough; it was just as important to know the why.

"Did you know," he asked, "that the diameter of the rim is twice the diameter of the ball?"

"Well…no Coach, I didn't," I responded with a touch of amazement. I suddenly realized he was trying to get me to visualize just how much space is actually available for a basketball going through a hoop.

"So," he went on, "if you think about it, it makes more sense to put an arc on your shot. That way, you give yourself more of a chance for the ball to drop into that open space in the hoop than you would if you shot the ball flat, with no arc."

There was the why, and it was so simple that I understood the concept immediately, but there was another problem. My shots were flat because I'd never bothered trying to shoot a basketball the correct way, even though I'd seen guys do it on TV all the time. The farther away I got from the basket, the worse it got. I explained to Coach that I just wasn't strong enough to do it correctly, or so I thought. Coach would hear none of that excuse.

"No, no," he said calmly, "I think you <u>are</u> strong enough; maybe not from 15 feet yet but you won't get stronger unless you focus on doing it correctly all the time. That will build your strength." I knew he was right.

"Here's one more thing that will help," he continued, "a lot of the power for a shot comes from the legs."

What? What's he talking about, I thought. You shoot with your <u>arms</u>.

"Do this," he said as he passed me the ball, "stand over here and shoot without jumping; just keep your feet on the floor."

We were about 10 feet from the basket. I turned to face the basket and, using correct form, I shot without jumping. The ball didn't make to the rim. He could sense my frustration.

"All right, all right, nobody hurt," he responded, with a phrase I would grow accustomed to hearing down the road.

As I went to retrieve the ball he continued, "Now come try it from the same spot but this time jump as you shoot."

"Remember," he reminded me, "You want to jump straight up and release the ball right at the apex of your jump."

I nodded my head as I thought through doing what he said. I dribbled the ball a few times and then jumped as I shot from the same spot as before. I missed the shot, but this time, the ball easily made it to the basket.

"Wow!' I said in amazement, "that felt good!"

"How about that?" he said with a grin that suggested a degree of satisfaction with my success. Then he added with a tone of conviction, "You keep working at doing it the right way every time and then it will become second nature to you. You'll be knocking down 15 footers in no time."

And that was it. In a matter of just a few minutes, Coach Trickler had made my day, and I was feeling very confident, believing maybe I did have a shot at making the varsity team one day.

Looking back, I can see clearly this was a Dave Boettger kind of moment. Here was another coach willing to take his own time to show me how to be better, to help me cross a threshold. Just like Mike Keville, Dave Boettger and Jett Colonna, Coach Trickler had a knack for making you feel like you mattered enough for him to mentor you in some way. Why would he bother to do that? What was in it for Coach Trickler?

Nothing actually, other than the pure satisfaction of taking his God given gifts and using them to help someone else. And when I doubted myself, as we all do at times, he pushed back in a positive way and kept encouraging me to just keep working at it, just as Dave Boettger had done.

This is what being a good role model looks like. This is how you mentor young men. What a gift. Fortunately for me, I was going to see a lot more of the same from him in the coming years.

In my 8th grade year, beginning in the fall of 1971, Coach Trickler was the head coach for JV football, and along with all 8th-10th grade boys, I was eligible to try out for JV football. I had yet to have a meaningful growth spurt at that point, so I decided to wait a year to try out even though a handful of my classmates did end up making the team. Still though, I desperately wanted to be involved, to be part of the team in some way. So, at the end of sports camp that summer, I talked to Coach Trickler.

"Coach," I said, "I know pre-season practices start in a couple of weeks. I'm not sure I'm ready to try out for JV this year. There's gonna be some big 10th graders on the team and I'm not sure I'm big enough yet. I know a couple of guys (8th graders) are planning to try out but I'm just not sure I'm ready."

He replied, "You know, I'm glad you've been thinking about it and it's not necessarily a bad idea to wait until next year if you don't feel ready. You're right, we've got some big guys this year and we should be pretty good."

Then, he ended by saying, "But, I'm counting on you being ready next year."

I wasn't expecting to hear that, but it sure sounded good to me.

"Yes sir, you can count on it!" I said.

"Good," he replied, "we're going to need you."

As was his habit, Coach finished the conversation on a positive note, which left me feeling very encouraged about the following season.

He then went on to say, "listen, you know the thought just occurred to me, we need a manager for this season. Is that something you might want to do?"

A manager is basically a "gopher" who takes care of things like making sure the water bottles are full or whatever task the coach deems necessary. But here's the upside: as manager, I would attend every practice and be on the sidelines for every game. At times it's a thankless job but it would give me the unique opportunity to soak up every bit of knowledge I could to help prepare me for the following season, when I would be trying out for the team. Not to mention the fact that Coach Colonna would be the assistant coach that season and bring his unique but necessary style of toughness to the team. I wanted to be a part of all that and so the decision was easy; I became the manager for the JV football team.

Thus began an incredible three-year ride, first as manager and then playing for two seasons under the leadership of Coach Dave Trickler. I had no idea what to expect when the season started that first year, but I was excited just to be part of the team in some small way. I had been playing intramural tackle football at NA every fall since 4th grade, but nothing had prepared me for how much I would learn from Coach during the three years I would be a part of the JV football team. All my previous intramural coaches had either been somewhat uninterested teachers pulling collateral duty, high schoolers earning community service credits, or students from Virginia Wesleyan College, whose campus was next to ours. Except for Coach Colonna my 7th grade year, all those early coaches were basically "playing out the clock" kind of coaches, just going through the motions. That's not how Dave Trickler did things.

Take, for instance, one of the first things I learned as manager my 8th grade year: every time we kicked off, we'd execute an onside kick......every time! Now I'm not sure what the odds for success are for onside kicks, but the simple fact is most, if not all teams at every level, only use onside kicks when they are desperate to keep the football. It's almost like a last resort and certainly not to be used on every kick-off! But that wasn't the case for the Norfolk Academy JV Bulldogs! But here's the thing: Coach Trickler did not take a cavalier approach to such a move. It served a purpose and the team practiced onside kickoffs nearly every day of practice; sometimes multiple times until they "got it right." How many teams do you know that do that?

As the guys on the kick-off team would line up to practice the kick, Coach would explain it.

"Now the other team knows we're gonna onside kick it and that's ok."

The first time I heard Coach say that I thought, "What are you talking about? I thought the whole point of onside kicks was the surprise element. And what if we don't recover it, which we probably won't?"

But then, he answered my question while I was still thinking about it.

"Remember, those guys on the receiving team are going to be really nervous, especially the ones on the front line, because they *know* it's coming.... everybody knows it! And they're just hoping the ball doesn't come to them. They also know if the ball *does* come to them, you guys are going to swarm all over 'em."

Every one of us could put ourselves in the shoes of the players on the receiving end of an onside kick. It wasn't difficult to picture being crushed trying to recover the kick and none of us would want any part of it. It all made perfect sense.

"Don't forget, because we practice it every day, until we get it right, our odds of recovery will be very good. And even if we don't recover it," he added, "I'm confident that Coach Colonna's defense will be strong enough to hold 'em."

We absolutely loved the gunslinger kind of attitude expressed by such a brazen approach. Yes, it was risky, but because we prepared so well, it wasn't careless. And it gave us a feeling that we believed we could do anything, and even if we happened to fail a time or two, we knew we'd be all right.

That philosophy was put to the test the first game of that 8th grade season. For what would turn out to be one of the few times all season, we didn't recover the onside kick. Our opponent promptly marched right down the field and scored. I then witnessed something I'd never heard or seen before. It took me a while to understand it. As our momentarily defeated defensive unit made its way back to our sideline, Coach Trickler greeted them by clapping his hands and shouting, "That's all right defense, here we go, nobody hurt, here we go!"

I was puzzled at first because I'd never seen a coach take such a positive approach to a negative outcome. But then I remembered he had said the same to me years earlier while teaching me how to shoot a basketball. I soon came to observe that perhaps Coach's most important gift of all was his understanding of the human psyche, especially for young male athletes. You could see the defensive players' body posture change with their heads held up higher as Coach let the defensive unit know, as well as the rest of the team, that everything was fine, that he still believed in us. We ended up winning the game.

"Hey Shep Jordan!"

It was a year later and Coach was calling to me from the other side of the gymnasium. It was one of the last days of the NA sports camp the summer before the start of my 9th grade year. By that time, I was a junior counselor at the camp and in a couple of weeks, both the varsity and JV football pre-season camps would be starting. Serving as the team manager for JV football the previous year had been a smart decision. This year though, I would be trying out for the team. I hustled over to where Coach stood.

"Hey Coach, what's up," I asked.

He said, "Hey, yeah, listen, we need to talk about this season."

I had been anxious to have this exact conversation.

He started by asking, "So, have you given any thought to what position you think you might want to try out for this year?"

I <u>had</u> been giving it some thought and even though I'd been a running back the previous two intramural seasons, I felt like I'd probably fit best on the line somewhere. I mean my dad and both brothers had been linemen so why would I not be one also?

Before I could respond though, he continued, "I've seen you've done a great job this summer in the weight room and getting your runs in. And you've finally started to add a little bulk to your frame." It felt good that he had noticed the work I had put in during my free time that summer.

"Thanks Coach," I said, "you know, I was thinking maybe I'd try out for offensive line this year."

"Yeah," he responded in agreement, "I was thinking the same thing. Listen, I have something I want you to consider."

I was about to find out that Coach Trickler was a consummate salesman, on par with being able to sell ice to an Eskimo or sand to a Moroccan nomad.

"What's that, Coach?" I asked.

"I really want you to consider playing center," he said with a touch of urgency.

There are arguably fewer positions in football more thankless than being the center. In my day, most teams lined up their biggest and sometimes toughest defensive lineman directly over the center, ensuring you would get a beating every game. Typically, the only time a center would get any recognition at all was if they screwed up somehow. But Coach had this knack for making you feel like your position was the most important on the field and without you, there would be no hope for success.

"Center?" I asked.

"Yeah," he said with a tinge of excitement, "I really believe you can make the biggest impact there."

He went on, "If you think about it, everything on offense starts with the center. We need someone totally reliable, and I think that you can be that guy."

Coach was saying all the right things and, of course, I was soaking up every word. I had once played center back in 6th grade and I always liked the idea of being the only one in that position (the rest of the offensive line is comprised of 2 guards and 2 tackles). I also liked having a degree of added responsibility by ensuring the offense would get back in the huddle in a timely fashion after each play. Playing center seemed like a good fit for me. But the truth was, there would have been no way I could say no to Coach Trickler. I trusted him implicitly.

"Sounds good to me, Coach," I replied, and it was settled.

Several weeks later, pre-season practice began. In my mind, I had finally arrived. My day had come. Like my dad and brothers had done before me, I would be putting it all on the line for the school team. I was a warrior; surely honor and glory would follow.

Mom liked to say, "Be careful what you wish for because you just might get it." Nothing in life to that point, not even having been the team manager the year before, had adequately prepared me for the physical and mental stress I endured during the week and a half of pre-season football practice. Coach Trickler had every second of practice time mapped out beforehand; there was never any standing around. He was like a maestro conducting an orchestra; every movement had a purpose.

We practiced twice a day, first in the morning and then

late afternoon for 8 days (we got the weekend off thank God!). It was grueling. The late August heat and humidity combined with helmets and pads made things sweltering. I used muscles I never knew I had.

Most of the team quickly fell into a daily routine. Once we got showered and dressed after the morning practice, many of us would head to the Lake Wright Hotel restaurant across the street from school to get some lunch, air conditioning and water. I remember the sympathetic waitresses would bring us pitcher after pitcher of water as we desperately tried to replenish the "gallons" we had lost during the heat of morning practice.

After lunch, we'd head back to school to congregate in the wrestling room. There, in the nice cool, dark space, we'd lie down on the soft wrestling mats to sleep and recover. At about 2:30pm we'd slowly rise and scramble back to the locker room, put on our practice uniform, still wet from the sweat of the morning practice, and head back out to the field for the start of afternoon practice at 3pm.

Yes, it was smelly and gross but that's just what warriors do, I told myself. As tough as those pre-season practices were, we knew that everything Coach threw at us was to prepare us for the battles to come. Another case of iron sharpening iron.

It's important to note that during my time as a student at Norfolk Academy, in any given year, there were roughly about 60 boys collectively in grades 8-10. Of those 60, a little over half made the JV football team each year. There is significance to this seemingly random statistic when you consider most of our opponents were the JV teams from the local public schools, who had a much higher number of boys to choose from. In other words, the public-school talent pool was much deeper than our own. It was inevitable that those teams would consist of players who were generally bigger, stronger, and faster than we were. Yet, in the two years I was a player, we only lost 2 games. In fact, under Coach Trickler's leadership, the JV football team regularly beat the public-school teams year to year. That level of success was in no way an accident or a fluke.

What then, was the "secret" to our success?

The "secret" wasn't a secret then nor is it a secret today. In fact, the "secret" is universal, timeless, and available to everyone. The one caveat however is that the "secret" must be learned and continually practiced in order to be effective. My fear is we are not actively teaching young men this valuable lesson these days. Fortunately for me and anyone who ever played for him, when it came to the "secret," Dave Trickler was a master teacher.

You generally think of a classroom as a place indoors with desks and a blackboard where you learned your subjects. Under Coach Trickler I came to understand that classrooms didn't necessarily need to have four walls or desks. Football fields and basketball courts are nothing more than classrooms as well. It was in these "classrooms" Coach Trickler taught his players certain truths: the key to competing successfully against any foe, no matter how big or talented they might be, is to be exceedingly thorough in preparation, fundamentally sound, and highly disciplined in execution. In short, preparation, fundamentals, and execution. To that end, we learned very early that nothing we did on the practice field was random. Everything was carefully planned out by Coach and designed to prepare us to be successful during games. He sold us on the theory that if everyone did their job on each play, we'd always be in a position to win. That theory proved to be true more times than not as in my two years as a player we won 10 games, lost 2 and tied once.

If you were to pick any one thing to showcase the incredible power and impact of the "secret" it would be the "belly pass." In fact, if you were to say "belly pass" to anyone who ever played on one of Coach Trickler's JV football teams, they would likely get misty-eyed with a smile of complete satisfaction on their face. Coach Trickler first started conjuring up this play, officially known as "strong right, fake 75, belly pass," when he was a high schooler playing quarterback at Prince George High School near Petersburg, Virginia. We all just called it the "belly pass," and over the years it became a thing of legend.

I can only speculate as to the degree of success the "belly pass" earned over the years but it must be close to 90% of the time it was run; maybe higher. So, with that degree of success, you might ask, why not just run it all the time? The answer has everything to do with preparation, fundamentals, and execution.

The ultimate success of the belly pass was dependent in large part on the consistent execution of another play, a running play called, "strong right, 75 belly." The "belly pass" always had the potential to be a knockout, game changing play. But just like everything in life with the potential for success, Coach taught us no great success in football or in life is ever achieved without first laying a solid foundation. The "75 Belly" was the foundation, the preparation, the set up for the "belly pass."

A simple, off tackle running play, the '75 Belly' was run to the left side of the offensive formation. There were two running backs who lined up in an "I" formation several yards behind the quarterback, one in front of the other. The quarterback would take the snap from center, turn to his left and fake a handoff up the middle to the first running back. The second running back would first take a jab step to his right and then come back left, take the handoff from the quarterback, and run off the left tackle. Seems pretty basic and it was, but Coach went to great lengths to teach us that it was the little details, the fundamentals, that would make this play or any play, successful or not.

"All right offense, listen up!" Coach would say as he started to teach us the "75 Belly."

The offensive unit would typically be lined up in formation on the ball and Coach would be directly across from us.

"Four yards," he'd say with emphasis making sure to make eye contact with each of us, "If we can gain just four yards every time we run the "75 Belly," we can then set up the "belly pass."

I remember in 8th grade when I first heard him say this it made little sense to me. Why just four yards, I thought? Don't we want to get as many yards as possible or even score on every play?

But then, of course, Coach explained the why, "First of all, if we can keep gaining 4 yards per play, we'll keep making first downs." I quickly did the math and realized he was right! Dang, I thought, I never looked at it like that! Coach was teaching us that the only way to eat the elephant in the room was one bite at a time. Somehow, he knew that a goal of gaining four yards on a running play was something we would see as very achievable, versus trying to "consume the whole elephant" every play. In our minds we could get four yards. It made so much sense.

But there was more to it.

He went on, "Plus, when we keep gaining 4 yards running the '75 Belly' they (the other team's defense) will soon become so focused on stopping it, they won't be ready when we eventually throw the belly pass at them. We'll have them right where we want them!"

It was an ah-ha moment for me and everyone else for sure. Coach was always so effective at clearly explaining what we were going to do as well as why we were going to do it. Let's be honest, if you're going to want a teenage boy to do anything, it better first make sense to him. Coach could put things into a perspective, like just get 4 yards, that made complete sense to us. However, understanding the theory and logic behind the set-up of the 'belly pass' is one thing but the execution of the play, having the ability to actually carry it out on the football field is another thing. The execution of the "75 belly" first and then the "belly pass" itself had to be nearly flawless.

To give us an edge in our quest to be flawless, Coach regularly engaged in something I'm pretty sure no other JV football coach did back then: he scouted our opponents. Scouting opponents is a common practice at most levels but typically not at the JV level. The reason is simply because it requires a degree of commitment of time and effort that most JV coaches are frankly not willing to give. But not Dave Trickler. Coach would use his exceptional selling skills to convince one of the other coaches, usually one of the Varsity team's assistants, to go watch the games of our upcoming opponents. That coach would then report back to Coach Trickler with valuable information about our opponent's tendencies, both offensively and defensively. Coach would then be able to prepare us with exactly what to expect from both the opposing team's offense and defense. That knowledge gave us a significant advantage and it went a long way to boosting our execution, especially against the public-school teams.

Coach continued to teach us the "75 belly."

"You have to sell the fake!" he implored, addressing the quarterback and two running backs.

And you have to go full speed every time, no going half speed," he continued, "otherwise, it has no chance to work."

Then he would turn his attention to the offensive linemen, "And O-line, you need to hold your blocks long enough for the running backs to do their thing."

We practiced the "75 belly" until, in Coach's eyes, we got it right. Then it was time to move to the "belly pass."

Coach continually assured us, "Once we've set it up with the "75 belly," the "belly pass" is going to work every time IF, everyone does their job!"

There's only one real difference between the "75 belly" and the "belly pass" but it's a big one. The quarterback, after faking the hand-off to the first back up the middle as usual, continues to his left where he would normally hand the ball off to the second back who would then run off tackle.

With the "belly pass" though, the quarterback instead fakes the handoff to the second back as well and keeps the ball himself. Now, if everybody's doing their job, selling the fakes, going full speed, and holding their blocks the defense will be swarming to the second running back, thinking it's another "75 belly."

This is where the quarterback has to be a great actor. He has to make it appear as though his role in the play is over and, while hiding the ball on his hip, he casually pivots blindly to his left and towards the right sideline. Meanwhile, the tight end, who lined up on the right side of the line of scrimmage has hustled to his left as though he were looking to block someone. At just the right moment, he breaks off, cuts back, and proceeds downfield towards the right side of the field where there is usually no defender anywhere in sight. At that point, the quarterback would come to life again, sprinting to the right also. It was a simple throw and catch from quarterback to tight end at that point, usually resulting in a touchdown.

Preparation, fundamentals, execution: the "secret" blueprint for success not just in football but for life.

In the previous chapter I outlined my path after graduating from Norfolk Academy in 1976. In early 1990, my divorce was finalized. And with two young sons at the time, I thought it best to try to stabilize, as best I could, an unstable family situation. So, I decided to leave a promising career in the Marine Corps, where I could be sent who knows where at a moment's notice. I took terminal leave from the Marines in early March, moved back to Virginia Beach and moved in with my parents.

I wouldn't say that I was at rock bottom at that point in my life but I sure could smell it. About a month after moving back, I decided to return to the Norfolk Academy campus to watch a varsity boys lacrosse game. I had not been back to the campus in many years.

It was a nice, sunny, early spring day and I thought it might do me some good to get outside and take in some fresh air. For some reason it didn't dawn on me that I might actually run into somebody that I would have to talk to. At that point in my life, I was feeling a profound sense of failure and I wasn't in the mood for any conversation about how I was doing; I just wanted to watch the game.

At least that's what I told myself.

Walking out to the field from the parking lot I realized that my desire for solitude was a pipe dream, especially when I saw that Coach Trickler was at the game. It was unavoidable; I'd have to talk to him. I have no idea how long it had been since I'd seen or talked to him, but it had been a while.

That didn't matter.

"Hey Shep Jordan," he shouted when he saw me.

Honestly, if I had to run into anybody that day, I would have picked Coach Trickler and maybe, subconsciously, that's exactly what I hoped would happen. By then he was the school's Athletic Director and still coaching boys Varsity basketball. Somehow, I knew that no matter what, I'd feel better in some way by talking with him. I was actually glad to see him.

"Hey Coach."

We shook hands and he said, "I heard you were back in town."

How did he know?

"Yep," I replied, with a sigh, "I'm back."

"Well, you're looking good," he said.

"Thanks Coach," I replied, "I'm doing Ok."

Then he quickly changed gears and asked, "Hey, remind me, how old are you now?"

What's he up to, I thought?

"I'm 33 now Coach." He shook his head in acknowledgement and continued, "Yeah, listen, have you given any thought about what you might want to do?" I suddenly felt as if it were twenty years earlier and he was asking me about what position I was trying out for on JV football. This time, Coach meant what was I going to do for a living?

"Well," I began, "I'm still on the government dole until May," referring to the fact I was on terminal leave. "But I've been thinking I'll probably try to get a position in finance somewhere;

I think I'd like to be a stockbroker." As I mentioned in the previous chapter, at that time income potential was my main focus and motivation.

He nodded his head as I shared my plan with him but as I was talking, he got a look on his face that I'd seen many times before. It was just like when he was selling me on trying out for center on the JV football team. His look was focused and I could see he was listening intently but I also knew he had something else on his mind.

"That sounds great," he said and I sensed there was a "but" coming and he didn't disappoint.

"But listen," he asked, "have you ever considered teaching and coaching?"

I knew what was coming next: the pitch. Just like he had done 30 years prior in convincing me how wonderful it would be to be a center on the JV football team, he was about to extol the virtues of a career in education.

"Well, no Coach, I haven't," I replied feebly.

He seized the moment, "Oh, man, well I think you would be great!"

"Uhh, I'm not so sure of that Coach," I muttered.

He had caught me off guard and I was searching for a way out.

"No, I'm serious," he continued, "We need guys just like you to teach and coach. I think you could make a big impact!"

Where had I heard comments like that before? But in my mind, I'm thinking, no way I'd go into education; there's no money in it.

So, I countered with this, "Well, you know I didn't play sports in college so I couldn't be a coach..."

Before I could even finish getting those words out, he countered with, "No, no, listen, it's not all about the X's and O's (coach speak for the ability to understand a sport) at this level. It's about being able to motivate the kids in a positive way." I was immediately struck by the reality that he had been the perfect role model of that very thing for me and countless others.

And then I said something that I regret to this day. I blame the lapse on my fragile state of mind back then.

"I don't know Coach; you know you don't make much money in education."

And there it was, my true motivation. Not once did I stop to consider that I was saying to a man I respected and admired that what he had chosen to dedicate his life to had no value, at least in the monetary sense.

He didn't blink an eye.

"Oh, I know!" he said with a laugh, "That's not the point though. We need guys like you in education right now. I really think you would be great. Will you just think about it?" Once again, Coach was saying all the right things.

"Ok Coach," I agreed, "I will."

"Good!" he said and smiled. We shook hands again and he slapped me on the shoulder saying, "It's good to see you!"

"Thanks, Coach, you, too."

Yet again, I left a conversation with Dave Trickler feeling better because of it. It's exactly what I needed to hear at a time when absolutely nothing felt good for me. As the best role models and mentors have a knack for doing, in the course of just minutes, Coach had built me up and made me feel as if I mattered, as if I had value. Not once did he refer to what I had recently been going through in my life, only to the possibilities ahead. Great role models and mentors don't dwell on the losses or the failures. They only urge you on towards greatness and then provide whatever tools and support they can to help you get there.

As you know, I eventually followed Coach's advice. He was right all along; education was the right fit for me. How did he know? Good mentors just know.

During my years in education, I worked at two of NA's rival schools so I would usually run into Coach several times during a school year at athletic events. It was always like running into a beloved family member.

Coach Trickler retired in 2001. Basketball was always his number one sport and in 35 years of coaching he won 573 basketball games and two state championships. Remarkable. His many other accolades and accomplishments are too numerous to mention. But you never would have heard about any of them from him.

It wasn't until I started working on this book that I realized I knew nothing about Dave Trickler's life before Norfolk Academy; nothing about his upbringing or the early influences on his life. He'd been an influential part of my life a long time; since 6th grade. But all I knew about him was "limited" to that time span.

At some point in late 2019, during a period where I was somewhat seriously working on this book, I decided I needed to catch up with Coach and hopefully have him fill in some of the blanks about his early life. He'd had a stroke several years earlier which hampered his speech to a small degree but I'd heard he was working out in a gym several days a week and trying to take care of himself.

"Hey Coach, its Shep Jordan," I announced when he

answered the phone.

"Hey buddy!' he responded enthusiastically, "How are you doing?" I could hear the effects of the stroke in his voice but the delivery was the same as always, positive and upbeat.

"I'm doing great Coach, thanks," I replied, "I hope you are, too."

"Yeah," he said, "This damned stroke is a pain but I'm otherwise Ok. I'm going to the gym twice a week!" he proclaimed with a degree of excitement.

"That's great Coach," I responded with an equal dose of excitement. He sounded good. The stroke may have slowed him down but it seemed he still had the same enthusiasm as the time he taught me how to shoot a basketball in 6th grade.

"So," he asked, "What's this thing you're working on?"

I proceeded to tell him about the book, what it was about, the message I was trying to send to all males but particularly young males, and his part in the collective story.

"I think that sounds great," he responded as I finished the explanation, "I'd love to help. But listen, I'm out of town right now and won't be back until Wednesday. Give me a call then and we'll set up a time to meet."

"Sounds good Coach," I responded, "I can't thank you enough!"

"I look forward to it," he said, "talk to you soon."

I had no way of knowing that would be my last conversation with Coach Trickler.

I did call him back the following week but got his voice recorder. I'm thinking he was probably at the gym! I left a message and asked him to give me a call when it was convenient. I never heard back from him and, to my regret, I never followed up. Not long after, I got sidetracked with something far less important that I allowed to take my focus away from working on the book.

I honestly don't remember how I heard of Coach's passing in August of 2020, I just remember how angry I was with myself. There was sadness also, to be sure, but I was angry that I had let yet another important person in my life slip away before I'd had a chance to tell them of the immense gratitude I felt for their positive, indelible impact on my life.

But, in his passing, Coach once again served as a motivator for me. I was faced with the stark reality that in my inconsistent efforts in writing this book I had fallen far short of one of the important elements of the "secret" that I had learned from Coach: execution. In the depths of my soul, I could picture him looking at me with an expression of concern bordering on disappointment.

"C'mon," I can hear him saying, "you're better than this! Let's go, let's get back to work!"

You see, there comes a time when all good mentors are no longer with us, but the truth is, they never really leave as long as we remember them and the lessons they taught us.

So, with a renewed commitment to finish this book, I remembered I still needed to have some knowledge about Coach Trickler's past, his upbringing. I reached out to Dave's three children, Stefanie, Brian and Tyler to see if they could fill in some of the blanks about their dad's early years. What they shared was frankly not what I had expected. Nevertheless, what I learned was incredibly enlightening and, to some degree, continued a common thread in the stories of all my men.

Influences and influencers play a critical role in the development of any child. This is particularly true in the story of

Dave Trickler and the first ten years of his life formed a unique foundation for a life that would ultimately have a positive impact on countless others.

Dave was born in Cincinnati, Ohio in 1943, at the height of World War II. His dad was career Army and at some point, after the war, the Tricklers were stationed in Japan. Can you imagine being a young boy, under 10 years old, living on an Army base in a country that your own country had recently defeated in war? It had to be challenging.

But I believe this is where Dave first learned to use his amazing people skills. He loved to tell his kids the story of sneaking off the base through a hole in the fence so he could go play baseball with some of the Japanese kids that lived nearby. Somehow, he convinced the locals to let him in the games.

I also think this was a time period where Dave's humble nature began to germinate. Instead of his first memories being of a comfortable home on a tree lined street in suburban USA, surrounded by kids who looked and acted just like him, he was an outsider. Plus, he was a witness to the reality of a country still trying to rebuild itself after a devastating world war. Dave learned early on that life can be challenging and sometimes unfair, but I think those early experiences molded him.

When Dave was 10 years old in 1953, his family moved back to the United States from Japan. His dad was stationed at Fort Lee in Prince George County, Virginia, where they remained through Dave's high school years.

Like many teenage boys searching for an identity, Dave found his through sports. Despite his innate natural abilities, he realized early that his lack of size would be something he needed help overcoming. He knew his athletic ability would take him only so far without that help and this is when the seeds of a future coach and mentor were sown. Instead of letting his height deficiency hold him back, he began to embrace the elements of the "secret." He learned how important it was to size up opponents to ensure he was prepared for what they might throw at him. He understood the importance and necessity of teammates so he learned how to motivate and bring out the best in his teammates. He came to understand that preparation, sound fundamentals and execution could help make up for any deficiency. Had he been 6'2" Dave Trickler's path in life might have been completely different. He likely would have gotten by on talent alone and not needed to invest so much time and effort into the "secret."

In the previous chapters, I could only speculate as to the impact the fathers had on their respective sons. It's important to note that Dave's kids were able to confirm that his relationship with his father was strong one. That news didn't surprise me. As a member of what's been called the Greatest Generation, Dave's dad reflected many of the men of that era. As described by his grandson Brian, William Trickler was "the salt of the earth, typical of that greatest generation, soft-spoken, humble, kind, and possessing the type of integrity no one would ever question."

Dave Trickler was one of the lucky ones and, by default, so are all of those he coached and mentored over the years. Lucky because he had a father who modelled for him what it means to be a man, a good man. Lucky for all of us who had Dave in our lives because he lived and modelled those same qualities.

So, let me ask you, what does success look like if you're a male in our culture?

That can be difficult to answer because success can be measured in any number of ways, like the way I was initially judging success after I left the Marines. These days the world measures success, especially for males, in ways that are shallow and, in the words of King Solomon from the Book of Ecclesiastes, "utterly meaningless." Money, possessions, and status are just a few of the barometers we have come to use to determine one's level of success. By his example, Dave Trickler, like all of my men, showed me that true success goes far deeper than those superficial benchmarks the world uses.

In chapter 12 of the Book of Romans, the Apostle Paul lays out a pretty simple blueprint for living a good, successful life. One of the earmarks of true success, according to Paul, is to serve one another with the gifts God has endowed us with. By that measure, Dave Trickler achieved what I would call eternal success. I've no doubt that Dave was proud of his measurable accomplishments, and there were many.

But I believe what he valued the most were the relationships and experiences along the way; the countless lives he touched and impacted. He made us all a little better than we would have otherwise been. Isn't that what really matters?

Dave Trickler - 1978

6

Royce Jones

"When the Great Scorer comes to mark against your name, He marks not whether you won or lost, but how you played the game."

Grantland Rice, early 20th Century sports columnist

"They gave it all they had, and what more can you ask? That's what it's all about, isn't it?"

Coach Jones

At some point in your life you've probably played a game of Simon Says. You know how it works: someone (Simon) is the leader and they tell you what to do and you then do it. Typically it goes like this, "Simon says touch your nose," and you touch your nose. Simple right? The challenge though, is that Simon doesn't have to do what Simon says to do. So, as long as you do what Simon says to do you stay in the game. But what if Simon touches his nose and says, "touch your nose?" Well, if you go ahead and touch your nose then you're out of the game because Simon didn't say "Simon says touch your nose."

It's a piece of cake really; you just have to stay focused.

But when Royce Jones was Simon, you were in for the ride of your life. And the crazy thing is, he only used two, sometimes three commands. To this day, I still don't know how he did it.

For seven summers beginning in 1969 (after my first 6th grade year) I was a camper first and later a counselor at the Norfolk Academy Day Camp. The camp was run by Royce Jones who taught English and Physics at NA and also served as the school's athletic director and head varsity football coach. With the help of Dave Trickler and a host of other coaches and teachers, the NA Day Camp was an incredibly fun way to spend summer days. It was made even better by the fact Royce's two sons, Chip and Craig, my "brothers from another mother," were also in attendance. Those seven summers were some of the best in my life.

Each day, the entire group of campers, roughly 60-70 kids as well as all of the counselors would congregate in the gymnasium in the afternoon before leaving for the day. Campers would sit on the floor in rows while announcements were made.

One of the highlights each week was the Friday, end of the day game of Simon Says led by Coach Jones. I confess, in seven years I never even came close to winning. Even now, I still shake my head thinking about it.

"Ok, here we go, everybody stand up!" Coach began.

There was always a high degree of excitement and anticipation before the start of each game.

"Ok," I said to myself, "This time I'm just not gonna watch him. That'll give me a chance."

But then Simon (Coach) said, "Simon says watch me."

At that point, I knew I was doomed, yet again.

After that initial command to watch him, thereby sealing my fate, Simon began, "Simon says do what I say, not what I do."

It started the same way EVERY time.

"Simon says arms up….Simon says arms down."

Coach would repeat this same command at least three to four times and each time he would do what he said to do. It was like he was signaling a touchdown. He went slowly at first, lulling us into a false sense of confidence. But then, it would get serious.

"Simon says arms up…Simon says arms down," the commands were coming a little quicker.

And then, "Arms up!!!" at which point Coach would raise his arms up with a look of urgency. Invariably, almost half the campers, lulled into a false sense of confidence, would be out.

Raising their hands with Simon, they failed to remember to do only what Simon said to do.

Coach would get this big grin on his face as the disgruntled kids sat down.

Then he would continue.

"All right…pay attention," and he would pause for a millisecond, "arms up!" Once again he would raise his arms emphatically.

Ha! Not falling for that one again! We were on to him at this point.

And then, seizing on our momentary triumph, he followed with, "*Simon* says arms down."

As he was putting the emphasis on the "Simon," he raised his arms yet again, and about another third of the campers that were left were eliminated because they raised their hands with the unconscious certainty the command would be "arms up."

As more kids sat down, Coach just giggled. It always looked like he was having the most fun of all.

At that point, and I usually made it that far, Coach would ramp it up. What ensued was always a marvel to behold. Coach would call out commands in a rapid, measured fashion, sometimes following his commands, sometimes not. He never missed a beat. How difficult is that? Well, if you've ever tried to pat your head with one hand while rubbing your stomach with the other, you have a sense of how challenging it is to do two separate things at one time. How Coach was able to effortlessly call out commands that he sometimes followed, sometimes not, was a special talent.

Typically, when it got down to only a handful left in the game, he would start throwing in a "Simon says arms out," into the mix, making it even more challenging to keep up. Most games, he just wore us down to the point where we would lose focus and eventually follow the wrong command. The crazy thing is, even though only one person could win, the rest of us "losers" still loved playing the game every week. Somehow Coach had a knack for making it incredibly fun, even as we went down in defeat every week. We loved it.

I first became aware of Royce Jones when I began attending Norfolk Academy in the fall of 1966. Despite the fact I was only a fourth grader, I knew full well he was the school's athletic director and head varsity football coach. Football was the "king" of the fall athletic season back then and whenever there was a Friday afternoon home game, my mom, sister and I would stay after school to watch the game. As a young boy desperately hoping to one day follow in the footsteps of my father and two older brothers as a football player, I soaked up every minute of each game. And I dreamed about the day I would don the school's orange, blue and white uniform and go to battle myself.

My dad rarely talked about things from his past but one of the things he had no problem talking about was Howdy Myers, his beloved high school football coach. Those stories led me to believe that a head coach is someone to be revered and respected.

Of course, as a young boy I didn't understand that those qualities had to be earned.

But I remember what dad had to say about Royce, "They've (the school) got a good one there in Royce Jones."

I figured dad knew what he was talking about so I kept listening.

"You know, he's a VMI (Virginia Military Institute) man and he was a star football player and also ran track."

Dad had great respect for VMI men. His uncle was a graduate and World War II hero and a number of his closest friends were also graduates. Dad's accolades had me convinced before I ever set foot on campus that Royce Jones must be someone special. Over the course of the next thirty years, I would learn many times over that dad had been right.

The first thing I remember about Coach Jones is that he looked like something out of central casting in Hollywood. Tall and fit with close cropped jet-black hair and a square jaw, he, as with each of the men in this book, had a commanding presence. He just looked like what you thought a football coach should look like. But he had more than just the right look.

You might have heard the old saying that goes something like this, "To whom much has been given, much will be expected; and from the one who has been entrusted with much, more will be asked."

Those words were uttered by Jesus as told in Luke 12:48. For me, this is lesson number one that every male needs to understand and embrace. Unfortunately, I'm seeing that there are fewer and fewer men living by these words today. Or should I say men willing to step up to that challenge.

Here's my point: you don't need to be a biblical scholar to know that each of us, every single human alive, has skills and talents that are unique to us. Things we can do as well or better than almost anyone else. How you choose to use those talents and gifts says everything about your character. Then there are those few people in the world who have been gifted with an innate ability to do everything well. Royce Jones was one of those people and how he used those talents is a testament to his upbringing and character.

Originally from North Carolina, the Jones family moved to Hampton, Virginia during the Depression years, hoping to improve their lot in life. As members of the Pentecostal Holiness Church, everything in their life revolved around their strong Christian faith. As the fourth out of six kids in his family and third out of five of brothers, Royce grew up in an environment where the things this world would claim are valuable didn't necessarily hold much value in the Jones's house. Royce's dad had a barber shop and he also grew produce that he would sell to help make ends meet. They lived in what would be considered the less affluent part of town.

By the time he reached high school, it was clear Royce had better than average ability musically, athletically, and academically. And he pursued each religiously. While at Hampton High School, Royce sang in the school chorus (where he would meet his future wife, Margaret), and learned to play the trombone proficiently. He excelled in the classroom and was not only a star on the football field but in track as well.

His son Craig shared with me once, "Believe it or not, dad was actually better at track than he was in football. He was lightning fast and that's what made him a good defensive back in football."

Royce was the co-captain of Hampton High's state championship football team in 1950 and it was his football and track talent that gave him the opportunity of a lifetime. College wasn't seen as a necessity in the Jones family especially since paying for that kind of education was beyond their means. Royce would need a scholarship if he were to continue on after Hampton High. VMI came calling and Royce answered the call and went to Lexington, Virginia, the first in his family to attend college. He continued to excel. He was elected Vice President of the Class of 1955 and was a cadet lieutenant. He played in the Regimental Band and he lettered in both football and track. He studied biology with the thought he might like to be a doctor one day.

By graduation day in 1955, the lure of medical school had waned and Royce and Margaret decided to get married and start a life together. Royce got a job as a patent examiner with the United States Patent Office in the Washington, DC and they moved to nearby Alexandria, Virginia. He would spend a little over four years in the Patent Office before an unexpected phone call led him to his life's calling.

At some point during those four years Royce got a call to see if he might be able to help coach football at Episcopal High School (EHS), a prominent, private boarding school for boys (now co-ed) in Alexandria. It was a part time gig but it eventually led to another full-time opportunity and Royce never looked back. After leaving the Patent Office he spent one year teaching and coaching with Bill Yost, of "Remember the Titans" fame at F.C. Hammond High School in Alexandria.

Then in 1961, he got another call, which would bring him to Norfolk Academy.

Early in the football season of my 10th grade year (1972) I was presented with an unexpected challenge.

As those of us on the Junior Varsity (JV) football team were warming up for practice one day, Coach Trickler called for me.

"Hey, Shep Jordan!"

"Right here, Coach," I responded as I hustled over to find out what he wanted.

"Listen," he started, "At the end of practice today Coach Jones wants you to come up (to the varsity practice) and do some punt snapping."

"Really," I said, surprised, "How come?"

"Don't know," he responded although I think he probably did.

Among the many things I learned from Dave Trickler was the proper technique for snapping the football for punts and field goal attempts.

"Think of it as though you're passing the football, but between your legs instead of standing up. Use your left hand to help control the ball as you snap it. Just remember to keep your butt low and follow through, almost as if you are pointing to the target as you release the ball," he explained, and I got to be pretty good at it.

At the end of JV practice that day I nervously made my way over to the varsity practice area. I remember trying to blend in unnoticed as I got there but that was wishful thinking. I was about to be put to the test and the entire varsity team knew it.

"Ooooohh, here comes JV boy."

"Hey Jordan! All eyes are on you my man."

"Don't screw this up young pup!"

You get the gist. Even though I knew every player on the team well, I was nonetheless being put through the gauntlet. But why?

Coach Jones walked over to me with a look that showed zero emotion and handed me a ball, "Here you go." He then moved about 5 yards directly in front of me. Everybody was watching.

"Ok," he said, "Let's see you snap a couple."

My "brother" Chip Jones was a senior and in his third year as the starting quarterback for the team. He was also the team's punter and as I looked around to see if he was ready he gave me the "you got this" look which is exactly what I needed.

"All right," I said to myself, still unsure of what this was all about, "Nothing to this, you've done it a hundred times."

I got into my stance and reached down to grab the ball. At that instant, as I was trying to concentrate on using proper technique, a size 11 foot wearing coaching shoes was suddenly planted about 6 inches from the ball.

It was Coach Jones.

While I was intently focusing on making a good snap, Coach had snuck up on me and was now directly over me. All I could see was his shoe but I knew it was him.

In my adolescent mind I was thinking, "Holy shit, it's Coach!"

That first snap to Chip was ok but not my best. I was a little tight. By the time I had made the snap and come out of my stance, Coach had moved back to his original spot 5 yards away. His facial expression remained unchanged.

"One more," he said, and Chip threw the ball back to me.

As I got back down in my stance and prepared for the next snap, the size 11 showed up again. This time though, my snap was strong and true.

Using my nickname Chip responded with, "Attaboy Shempsk!" The rest of the team started to buzz with conversation.

"Last one!" Coach commanded and yet again, the size 11 was my unwanted companion. My last snap was another good one. Clapping ensued from the otherwise uninterested players.

"Ok...good job," Coach said, "You can head on in."

As I headed into the locker room, the varsity team remained to finish up the rest of their practice and I wondered what had just happened. The varsity already had a good punt snapper in Ricky Glover, a senior who was a two-way starter on both the offensive and defensive line.

The next day as I was on my way to lunch I heard, "Hey, J Shepherd!" That was Coach's nickname for me.

"Hey Coach," I said thinking maybe he would let me in on the reason behind the previous day's adventure.

He got right to the point, "I had an idea and yesterday was your audition. Here's what we're going to do. For the rest of our home games, I want you to dress out with the team and do the long snaps for punts."

Although I had a sense this might be where it was all going, I was still a little surprised.

"Who, me? Really?"

"Yes, really," he said without hesitation, "I already knew you were a good long snapper and yesterday you handled the pressure we put on you pretty well. I'd rather give Ricky a break from special teams if we can so we'll see how it goes."

"Ok Coach."

"Good," he replied, "So you'll still practice with the JV every day but you'll be with us on home game days."

I didn't know what to think. My mind was going berserk.

Dressing out with the varsity was great but I never really felt as if I was part of the team. To begin with, there weren't enough varsity uniforms so I had to wear my JV uniform on game days, and this naturally made me stand out from the rest of the team. Plus, I was still the starting center on the JV team so I never practiced with the varsity. I did get in a handful of snaps during a couple of the home varsity games but by the last game Ricky Glover took all of the long snaps.

By the end of school that year, Chip was getting ready to graduate and preparing for a June departure to attend the Naval Academy. Meanwhile Craig and I signed on for another summer working at Day Camp. We were really going to miss Chip. He had been a fixture at NA for 12 years and he had left an indelible mark on the school.

Right before the end of school, I ran into Coach in the gymnasium.

"Hey, J Shepherd!" he said enthusiastically.

"Hey, Coach, what's going on?' I replied.

"Have you heard?" he asked.

"Heard what?"

There's another Chip Jones coming to school in the fall," he said with a sly grin.

I was totally confused.

"What? What do you mean?"

Coach started to giggle, "Yeah, can you believe it? He's a Navy kid and he and his family are moving here this summer. He'll be a senior."

Naval Station Norfolk is the largest naval complex in the world so Navy families are coming and going all the time. Consequently, it wasn't unusual that this "new" Chip was coming in for his senior year.

But I wasn't picking up on why Coach was telling me this.

So I asked, "Is he a football player?"

"You bet he is, and he's got good size." He paused for a split second and then looked at me and smiled as he revealed, "Oh, and by the way, he plays center, too."

Since the day Coach Trickler "convinced" me to play center back in 9th grade, I had never been challenged by anyone seeking to unseat me as the starting center. I mean who in their right mind really wants to play center? I admit that my teen-aged mind had simply assumed the position would always be mine simply by default. And with the impending graduation of the varsity center, Lee Moore, I figured I would naturally just follow in his footsteps.

"Seriously?" I responded with a hint of disbelief and disappointment.

"Yep!" said Coach, "Gotta run, see you later."

It seemed to me that Coach was strangely happy about the news he'd just imparted to me. If you don't count my brief tenure as a punt snapper the previous fall, I had not yet been on a team coached by Royce Jones but our relationship had grown strong by that point. I spent almost as much time with Chip and Craig at the Jones house as I did my own. Couple that with the years working with Coach at Day Camp, and by the start of my junior year, I had become an unofficial member of the family. Coach had become somewhat of a father figure to me. But now that I was heading to the varsity team, my relationship with him was understandably taking on a whole new dynamic.

Later that summer I actually met the "new" Chip Jones and he turned out to be a really nice, personable guy. But at 6'2" and probably 220 pounds, he outweighed me by almost 30 pounds.

In retrospect, I was too immature then to understand what Coach was doing, not only in that initial 30 second conversation about the new Chip Jones, but also the punt snapping experiment the previous fall. It was so subtle and yet I didn't realize it until much later. What he was doing was preparing me for the challenges ahead of me as I moved to the varsity level.

"You're going to be challenged this year," he was saying

without saying it, "And it's going to be tough. Just because you started on JV for two years doesn't mean you automatically start on varsity." In other words, "you're going to have to earn it."

Looking back, I'm sure the reason Coach seemed happy about the new Chip Jones is because he knew that I, like every young male, underlined needed to be challenged. I needed to have to work hard and strive for something that I wanted very badly versus just having it handed to me. Challenge is a powerful motivator and he knew it. It wouldn't be the last time Coach tested me in that way.

Years later, Coach confided in me, "You know I never intended on Chip (the new one) playing center. I really wanted him to anchor the defensive line at nose tackle (the defensive player directly across from the center). But I wasn't about to let you know that!"

I looked at Coach with a "are you kidding me?" look.

"Coach," I said with a hint of exasperation, "Chip and I battled EVERY day in the blazing August heat and humidity during pre-season camp that year. I don't mind telling you, it was brutal!"

"I know!" he said as he broke into a big grin that reflected the satisfaction of a plan that had worked.

And then he got serious and said to me in a caring, fatherly tone, "You needed to show me you could step up to the challenge. More importantly, you needed to show yourself, too. Honestly, Chip probably got the better of you early on but the thing is, you got better and came back stronger every day. By the end of camp it was basically even between you two and that's all I needed to see."

One of the most difficult things for any role model and

mentor to do is challenge their charges to reach higher than they think they can go. These days, fear of failure is getting in the way of young men learning how to face challenges and learning to work hard to achieve success. Failure is necessary for success. And without challenge and the bravery to face potential failure, we breed men who are entitled and weak. As tough as it was to battle a guy bigger than me in the hot August sun, I'm eternally grateful Coach gave me that test at precisely the right time in my young life.

I'd earned my spot and I felt a strong sense of accomplishment. I started every game my junior and senior seasons.

Later that season, Coach did it to me again. It started with the scouting report for our upcoming opponent, St. Christopher's School from Richmond, Virginia. St. Chris was and is a big game for us every year. They were consistently a good, strong team and my junior season was no exception.

Coach started the scouting report by looking directly at me, "They've got a nose tackle who's not all that big."

"Phew, " I thought, "Finally a game where I'm not going to get pounded by some big lug."

"His name is Tommy Sotos. He was All-Prep last year and he's mean as a snake," coach said in his usual calm, matter of fact tone.

"Really?" I replied quietly, slightly stunned at the unwanted news.

"Not only that," Coach continued, "He's quick as a cat. He literally has the ability to disrupt everything we will want to do on offense."

"He's very unconventional. He'll randomly shoot the gap on either side of you almost every play."

In my day, defensive players were taught to first engage the offensive player in front of them when the ball was snapped. That's because very few defensive linemen were quick enough to shoot the gap between offensive linemen on one side of the line of scrimmage and still be able to run down the ball carrier running to the opposite side.

"But Coach," I implored, "Won't he take himself out of the play if he chooses the wrong gap?"

Coach smiled and said, "Yeah, you'd think so but Sotos is quick enough to make the play, even if he picks the wrong gap."

"Oh geez," I thought to myself, "Why me?"

I could tell from Coach's tone that he wasn't embellishing anything about Tommy Sotos. But there was not a hint of panic in his message to me and in fact there never was whenever he was laying out a significant challenge.

It was always the same message from Coach: acknowledge and accept the "steep mountain" in front of you, dig down and summon the resolve and courage to step up and face the challenge, and then do everything possible to meet the challenge successfully. This is how leaders lead and how role models teach young men to become strong men.

"We've got some things we're going to do in practice this week to get you ready," he continued.

I never once got the impression during this brief conversation that Coach felt like I wasn't up to the task. But then practice started.

Randy Thornton was a senior reserve defensive lineman that year and it was decided he would be Tommy Sotos during practice the week leading up to our game. At first I was grateful I wouldn't be banging heads with Chip Jones as was usually the case. But I soon learned there was a reason Coach had picked Randy. He was quick, kinda like Tommy Sotos, and not as big as Chip. A fairly accurate replica of what I was to face.

"All right offense, huddle up!" Coach called out.

It was the first day of practice (Monday) the week of our game against St. Christopher's. It turned out to be a long, frustrating week for me.

The first play was called and as we broke the huddle Coach yelled out, "Here we go!" I was tentative, feeling like the success or failure of our offensive effort that week depended entirely on my ability to block Tommy Sotos (and Randy).

Play after play, I was getting beaten easily by Randy's quickness. It was almost like he knew where each play was going. This went on for a couple of practices. Coach never got flustered and continued to encourage me even though it seemed I was not making any progress. But I sensed the rest of the team was starting to lose confidence in me. Then, on Wednesday, Coach called me over while the team was working on defensive stuff.

"I want you to try something today when we start working on offense," he started, "when you snap the ball, wait just a split second before you step off to make your block."

Offensive linemen had always been taught to fire off the ball at the snap so this advice from Coach didn't make any sense at first.

"Use that split second to get a sense of where Randy's going. All we need you to do is just get a piece of him, regardless of which way the ball is going. Doing that will slow him down just enough that he won't be able to get a clean shot at the ball carrier."

And just like that, the stress that had consumed me melted

away. We had a plan. The message was simple: you don't have to beat Tommy Sotos on every play, you just have to make it hard for him to make a play. Why hadn't Coach told me this on Monday?

The plan worked. For the last two practices before our Saturday afternoon game, I started getting a piece of Randy Thornton on just about every play. Maybe, I thought, I can do this?

Game day turned out to be a beautiful sunny fall afternoon for our home game. Tommy Sotos appeared to be everything he was advertised to be. As a team co-captain he led the Saints out to the field and I just remember he reminded me of the Tasmanian devil cartoon character from Looney Tunes, tightly wound and ready to bust loose. I don't know why, but I had a strange calm and felt remarkably little stress about the task at hand for me. Our whole team played well and we won the day. Tommy Sotos and I battled it out to what I would call a draw. At least on that day, he hadn't been the game changer that Coach had led us to believe he could be.

Years later, Coach and I reminisced about that week of practice. "Did you know," he began with his standard wry smile," every time the offense broke the huddle to go run a play, I would point to Randy which gap I wanted him to shoot?"

The coaches always stood with the offense when we were running plays so that when we broke the huddle they were behind us. I had no idea Coach was "stacking the deck" against me! No wonder I barely laid a finger on Randy those first two days of practice.

"Coach, really?" I said, shaking my head in mock disbelief.

"We had to get you ready and that was the best way. By

game time, you had seen enough of it in practice to be able to handle Sotos during the game."

"Man, what a tough week that was," I replied.

"Yeah," said Coach breaking out in another big grin, "but it worked, didn't it!"

Good mentors just know how to challenge you in a way that brings out your best.

Good mentors and strong men also show you their true character when things go badly and don't necessarily turn out the way they planned. My senior year, Royce Jones showed us all what's really important in life and it took a football game to reveal the timeless message.

Woodberry Forest School has been in existence since 1889 and like Episcopal High School where Royce got his start, it's an all-boys, private boarding school for grades 9-12 located near Charlottesville, Virginia. And just like EHS, Woodberry attracts students from all 50 states. Consequently, they typically have a deep, diverse pool of athletic talent to choose from. In my day, they were somewhat of a football powerhouse in the state of Virginia. My junior year (1974) they beat up on us winning 42-17, but we took solace in the fact we scored more points on them than any other team they played that year.

My senior season (1975), the Woodberry game was the next-to-last game on our schedule. Expectations had been high at the beginning of the season, but we had lost 2 heartbreakingly close games by a combined total of 7 points. In many ways, we felt "snakebit" by fate but the Woodberry game would give us the opportunity to make up for those losses.

As always, Coach approached this game like any other game: acknowledge and accept the difficult challenge, find the resolve and courage to face the challenge, and then do everything you can to meet the challenge.

Nevertheless, we started the game somewhat tentatively, almost as if we were trying too hard instead of just playing to our ability. In no time flat, two nervous turnovers led to easy Woodberry touchdowns and we were down 14-0 early in the game. Was this game going to be another blow out? Offensively, we never got farther than the Woodberry 33-yard line in the first half. Somehow though, we made it to halftime only down 14-0.

"Everybody ok, anybody hurt?" Coach started every half-time with these same two questions. It was almost as if he was saying, "Ok, everybody just take a deep breath and relax."

He waited about a minute or two so we could all get focused and then said, "Let's talk about what we're gonna do in the second half."

Not one word was said about the first half, the turnovers that had led to easy Woodberry touchdowns. There was no sense of panic, just a firm resolution about the task still ahead of us. Another hallmark characteristic of a great role model.

"Defense, you're doing a great job, don't let up. Offense, we need to get a better rhythm going so we're going to start running the ball more. Let's see what happens if we start pounding the ball at them."

Honestly, the mere thought of pounding the ball against a team as strong as Woodberry was a stretch. But Coach planted the seed and we bought into it. It also helped that we had Mike Newhall.

Mike was (and still is) a big, strong athletic guy who went on to play collegiately at the University of Virginia. He joined our class at NA as a 9th grader and made an immediate impact on the athletic fields and on the basketball court. By the time we were seniors he stood about 6′2″ tall and went about 215 lbs. He was a versatile athlete and he lined up as a fullback in our I formation offense. For the better part of the second half it was Newhall right, Newhall left and Newhall around the end. Midway through the half we drove 70 yards in 13 plays with Mike scoring on a 5-yard run. We were pounding the ball at them and it was working!

Then Coach did something unthinkable after the touchdown: we went for 2 points! Even though my "brother" Craig was an "all-world" kicker and nearly perfect on extra points that season, we went for it. Mike's run for the conversion was good and suddenly it was 14-8.

I didn't understand it then but I know now that Coach could see that we were on the verge of putting Woodberry on the ropes. They were getting worn down having to bring down Mike and going for two was a bold move but it just made sense.

We started to believe it was our day.

There were 11 minutes left in the 4th quarter when we kicked off after our touchdown. The defense had done a great job shutting down the Woodberry offense after their 2 touchdowns in the first half. They shut them down again and forced a Woodberry punt. We got the ball back on our own 45-yard line, great field position. But there was still a little more than 8 minutes left on the clock, an eternity.

Remember that Coach Trickler had always stressed the importance of gaining 4 yards on a play. That keeps the clock moving and also insures you keep making first downs. And so, we methodically began our march down the field, taking as much time off the clock as possible and gaining enough yardage each play to keep making first downs.

Once we got to the Woodberry 35-yard line Coach started calling sweep plays, one after another. Sweep plays are run to the far edge of the line of scrimmage towards the sidelines before the ball carrier turns to run up field. Consequently, they take more time off the clock which was the whole point. Mike was the ball carrier on the sweep plays and after about 5 sweeps to the right, we were at the Woodberry 2-yard line. The game clock kept ticking.

As we huddled up to call the next play, I looked at my good friend, left guard Danny Rumble and said, "Man, we're doing this! We're winning this game!"

The play call came into the huddle, another sweep right to Mike.

At the snap of the ball, I made my block and with the certainty of our impending touchdown, I looked back to the right end of the line of scrimmage, expecting to see Mike waltzing into the end zone. Suddenly, though, one of Woodberry's defenders rushed and met Mike head on at the line of scrimmage. They looked like two wild, big horned rams crashing into each other and the impact stopped the momentum of each player. As Mike reset himself and began fighting for yardage he lost control of the football and it fell to the ground. A Woodberry player recovered it. There was 1:40 left on the game clock but it was over.

Looking back, the loss of a high school football game would seem insignificant in the grand scheme of life. At the time, though, it was crushing. It was an early, painful lesson that life doesn't always turn out the way you would like it to. You certainly can't lay any blame on Mike who ran for 101 yards on 19 carries for the day. He had been instrumental in leading us to the point we could win.

Perhaps because of my mental state of mind when it was over, I have no recollection of what Coach said to us after the game. It was only the article in the newspaper the next day that spoke to the character of Royce Jones and what really matters in life.

Long before the internet and social media, the daily newspaper was THE source of news and information. The sports section of the newspaper would publish a roughly 150-word synopsis of each of the high school games that had been played the previous day and our game was no exception.

But there was another, much longer article, that the newspaper ran about our Woodberry game. Interestingly, it was written by Jeff Steckroth, who had been another one of my counselors at Camp Greenbrier. Jeff had been at the game and was struck by the drama of it all. As a highly decorated athlete himself while a student at Maury High School, he understood the significance of our loss. The title of his article was "Bulldogs shy by two yards." I want to share the last two paragraphs of the article, which made an indelible mark on my soul.

"Woodberry coach Red Caughon had nothing but praise for the Bulldogs and Newhall. 'They deserved to win. They outplayed us in the second half and they would have scored at the end if they hadn't fumbled. That Newhall is some kind of runner, a great competitor.'"

And then, "For the Bulldogs, now four and three, the loss was tough to take because Woodberry Forest is the twice-defending Prep League champ, and winner of 27 of its last 28 games. Jones, though obviously disappointed, was proud of his team's play. 'They gave it all they had, and what more can you ask? That's what it's all about, isn't it? Well, isn't it?'"

In those 22 words, Royce Jones showed his true character, the character of a good man. Life isn't necessarily going to be fair he was telling us, even when it seems you deserve better. What matters most, he was saying, even more than your won/ loss record is how you play the game, how you live your life, in spite of what is thrown at you. It's a message many unfortunately tend to ignore these days.

In 1979, Royce and Margaret left Norfolk Academy after 18 years to head back to Lexington, Virginia, and his alma mater, VMI. In 1980 he took the position of Director of Cadet Affairs at VMI, and this put him right back in direct, daily contact with the students. For the next 15 years Royce faithfully served both the VMI and local community in ways that are too many to list. And as they had so gracefully done during their NA years, Royce and Margaret always welcomed any and all into their home.

You know when the phone rings in the middle of the night that its most likely not something good. It was 2am on July 10th, 1995, when the phone rang.

"Uh-oh", I thought as the shrill of the phone woke me out of a deep sleep. "I hope it's just a prank call."

It wasn't.

"Hello," I said almost as a question, like maybe the caller had the wrong number. I spoke in a low voice, not wanting to wake anybody else up.

"Shep!" I knew immediately the caller was my "brother" Craig and I could hear the quiver in his voice.

"Craig? What's going on bro?" I asked, not really wanting to hear the answer.

He paused for a second and then said, "We lost dad."

His voice was breaking badly but I heard what he said and

I knew what he meant.

Nevertheless, I responded with, "What?!"

"Dad's gone man, it was his heart," he responded through tears.

"No!" I replied as my own heart suddenly became extraordinarily heavy, "No!"

"They took him to Stonewall Jackson (hospital)," he continued, "but he didn't make it."

And then, there was silence. I guess it was shock; I struggled to find words.

"Shep?" Craig asked.

"Yeah man, I'm here," I replied quietly as my own tears started to fall.

There's really no way to prepare for the sudden loss of someone who means so much to you. I'd already learned that lesson twice by that point in my life. In 1986, my brother Fred died suddenly at age 38, exactly two weeks before I had to leave on a six-month deployment while in the Marines. That was tough. Then, in 1990 (not a great year as you know by now) my sister-in-law, Roxanne, died after surgery to remove a brain tumor. She was only 42.

There's a certain pain you feel at times like these that is difficult to express in words but its intensity is unique and unmistakable. Even though I was already acquainted with it, it didn't help ease the pain of learning Coach was gone and gone way too soon. He was only 62 years old. Until that moment, I never consciously realized how important he had been in my life.

I was honored by the family to be asked to serve as a pall bearer at Coach's funeral. The service was a solemn yet grand gathering of folks from both the Norfolk Academy and VMI families. Coach had touched so many lives.

As we made our way to Lexington's Stonewall Jackson Cemetery and Coach's final resting place, I was desperately struggling with the stark reality of having to say goodbye to a man who had <u>always</u> been there for me, unconditionally, even when I had at times been distant. I agonized that I had not ever expressed my love and gratitude to him for his positive influence in my life. And now, it was too late.

As we carried Coach to his gravesite, I found myself at the foot of his casket on the right side. Once we leaned down and placed him in the right spot, I let go of the casket's handle.

But before I stood up to go to my seat, I reached out with my left hand, patted his casket, and whispered, "There you go Coach." It was an impulsive action I had not anticipated. It just happened. I'm pretty sure no one noticed and to be honest, I hope no one did. It wasn't a moment meant for anyone else but Coach and me.

If you've ever tucked your kids in at night, pulled their blanket up and given them a loving pat on their cheek, you know what I was feeling at that moment. It was my final thanks, my final expression of love and respect. I will cherish it the rest of my days.

The 1963 edition of the Norfolk Academy yearbook was dedicated to Coach. He was all of 30 years old and had only been at NA a couple of years, but he had already made his mark. The dedication reads,

"For keen insight into the problems of students,
For unfailing enthusiasm and strong leadership in
The classroom and on the athletic field,

Above all for his outgoing friendliness"

To whom much has been given, much will be expected. Royce Jones had the talent, personality and intellect to choose from any number of paths in life. Yet, he chose the path less traveled, the path of serving others, predominantly young people.

Over the years Craig has shared with me how his dad was always inspired by some of the great figures from the Old Testament of the Bible. People like David, Gideon, and even Moses and Joshua. All these men (and others) had one thing in common, they were reluctant to answer God's call on their lives. They were reluctant in the sense they basically believed themselves not up to the call God placed on their hearts.

How many of us have felt the same I wonder?

Yet, when these men eventually answered the call, marvelous things happened. There's a lesson for us all here and Royce Jones was an excellent example of the potential we all have of finding our purpose in the world. I think back to things like our weekly games of Simon Says and the pure joy and fun Coach seemed to be having as he was leading us. In fact, I can't remember a time where Coach wasn't upbeat and seemingly content with his role in this life, whether at NA or VMI. And the reason is clear: when you know in your heart that you are living the true purpose for your life, the one God's called you to, it shows. Its unmistakable. There's joy at the center of your life.

As with all the men in this book, it's hard to adequately quantify Royce Jones's impact on my life. Yet, I shudder to think of how differently my life would have been without his presence and influence. I know there are countless others who share the same feeling about him.

As we move to the next and final chapter on my dad, it's the appropriate time to start thinking about legacy, the long-lasting impacts you will leave behind. I'm not referring to the physical things necessarily, like money and possessions. They can be gone in an instant. I'm referring to the impacts you make that will last for generations to come, the impacts that time can't erase no matter how many worldly possessions you may have.

Royce Jones-1971

7

<u>James M. Jordan, III</u>

"Train up a child in the way he should go, and when he
is old, he will not depart from it"

Proverbs 22:6

"Old man, look at my life, I'm a lot like you were"

Old Man by Neil Young

It was sometime around 2018 that I first told my wife Mary Downey about my idea for this book. I had just finished explaining to her the overall concept for the book and the intent of its message when I revealed to her the men I planned to write about.

She noticed one person missing.

"What about your dad?" she inquired.

"What do you mean?" I responded quizzically.

"I <u>mean</u> what about your dad," she replied somewhat sharply, "why isn't <u>he</u> one of the men in your book?"

Mary Downey loved my dad; heck, everybody did!

I had no answer.

"Well," I muttered sheepishly, "I'm not sure."

The truth is, when I initially began working on this book, I did not intend on including this chapter on my father. Actually, it's more accurate to say the thought never occurred to me to include him. You might think that a little odd and I wouldn't blame you if you did. In an ideal world, a boy's father is typically the first and most influential role model in his life. I confess I'm slightly embarrassed and maybe even a little ashamed by that initial omission, but in retrospect, it says a lot about my relationship with my dad.

I'm grateful Mary Downey came to his "defense" because it got me to thinking. She was right, why wasn't my dad on the list? Shouldn't he have been the first name?

When I finally came to understand the reason dad had

been an afterthought it came as a bit of a surprise but then, as I thought about it more, it all began to make sense to me. You see, I had a great dad. He did just about all the things a good dad should do; he was a devoted and faithful husband, a steady provider for our family and a man of unshakable character and integrity. He was home every night. He came to all my athletic games. He had the best sense of humor and a laugh that was contagious. He was what we in the south call a true southern gentleman. In those ways, dad was a great role model for me and my siblings.

So, what was missing for me?

It was only after I started dissecting my relationships with the other men in this book that I came to realize that despite all of his marvelous qualities, for the better part of my life, but especially during those important early years, even though my dad was present in my life every day, he was nevertheless emotionally unavailable.

Now that's a pretty bold thing to declare, I know. Those who knew my dad might be a little surprised to hear such a thing because he was such an outgoing and friendly guy. Some might even be angry at me for the revelation. But don't get me wrong, I loved my dad and I miss him every day; but I can't deny there was a hole in our relationship that I never realized existed until I started to write this book.

So, in conducting a moderate degree of research on emotional absence I learned that being emotionally unavailable doesn't necessarily mean something is wrong with you. One of the things it <u>can</u> mean is that you are having to use so much of your emotional energy on your own circumstances and feelings that you don't have enough left for anyone else. You're going to see that's exactly what happened to my dad. He used up so much emotional energy throughout his life dealing with what life threw at him, that he didn't have much left for me at the time I needed it the most. But I didn't realize it or, more importantly, understand why until I started thinking deeply about the nature of role models and mentors.

Fortunately, as I began the process of putting the pieces of my dad's life together, so much became clear to me, and in that clarity came healing I didn't even know I needed. I embraced the truth that there is and never will be any male figure more important in my life than my father. And that's not just true for me; I believe that to be a universal truth for every man. My dad's story and what it reveals about the significance of a young male's relationship with his father as well as with the other male role models in his life, is a fitting and appropriate conclusion to this book.

How could I not include him?

Throughout the other stories in this book, I've tried to show not only how my role models and mentors impacted me, but also to shed some light, when possible, on what and who influenced them when they were young. To a certain degree, that knowledge is equally as important because good role models and mentors aren't necessarily born, in many ways it's a learned skill. Once I started digging into my dad's past to fill in the gaps of knowledge that were missing, an incredible and sometimes sad story unfolded which gave me keen insight but also a greater appreciation for him.

His is an important story because it clearly reveals that you just never know what life is going to throw at you and how the impacts affect not only you, but indirectly those you mentor as well. And sometimes, those impacts can span generations.

What I want <u>you</u> to do as you follow my dad's story, is to consider and embrace the reality of <u>your own</u> father's story and the impact it may have made on the man you are today. I understand that might be painful for some; to a small degree it was for me. But I'm convinced making that connection, having that knowledge is absolutely critical and necessary for your own development as an effective role model and mentor. Isn't that what's important here? And, who knows, maybe <u>you'll</u> experience healing you never knew you needed.

To fully understand the scope of my dad's journey and its impact on him as well as me, you have to go all the way back to 1911. That year, my great-grandfather James M. Jordan, Sr. came down with tuberculosis.

Dad never said much about his namesake but as a kid I had a natural curiosity about his grandfather. I remember asking him a couple of times what James, Sr. was like. Maybe, there was some great story about the patriarch of our clan he could pass on to me.

"Well," he would say, "you know, he was pretty old (61) by the time I came along."

It felt like he was searching for the right words to say but they just didn't come.

"I actually had a better relationship with my grandmother," he added. "She was somewhat younger and just a sweetheart."

I always found it odd that dad had so little to say about his grandfather. James, Sr. lived to the ripe old age of 84 so it's not that dad didn't have the time to make a connection with him. For whatever reason, dad and his grandfather apparently never formed a close bond.

At the time of his illness, James, Sr. was 52 years old and had a thriving insurance business, a wife and five children living in Norfolk, Virginia. My grandfather, of the same name, was the eldest son of the five children and 14 years old. These days TB is certainly not something to take lightly but in 1911 it was a much more serious condition. Consequently, James, Sr. was forced to stay home and recuperate for as long as it would take to get well, which understandably made a significant impact on the family's financial resources. He eventually had to declare bankruptcy, which naturally created a social "stain" on the family.

My grandfather, who all of us grandchildren called Big Jim, had just finished his 8th grade year at Norfolk Academy. He would never go back to school. As the eldest son and at the time technically old enough to work, he had little choice but to drop out, and go to work to try and help bring some income to the family. Fortunately, through his dad's business connections, Big Jim began working for a company where he would eventually become proficient in accounting and business management. These skills would serve him well later in life and help to provide for him a very comfortable lifestyle.

But nothing can replace the fact that circumstances outside of his control derailed his adolescence and limited whatever dreams he might have had to follow a path in life of his own choosing. What a harsh reality for any young male to shoulder.

Now, contrast that to Big Jim's younger brother, Irvine. My Great Uncle Irvine, who was four years younger than Big Jim, was able to follow his dreams, in no small part due to the sacrifice Big Jim made by going to work at 14 years old. Irvine was a graduate of the Virginia Military Institute (VMI), Class of 1924 and the Vice President of his class. Upon graduation, he took a commission as an officer in the United States Marine Corps and began a life that took him to far away places. Uncle Irvine first rose to fame in the summer before the bombing of Pearl Harbor in 1941. With the rest of the world already at war, he was en route to London where he would be the Assistant Naval Attaché at the American Embassy. But the ship he was on was torpedoed in the North Atlantic by a German U-Boat and he was one of just 8 Marines rescued. Later, in 1943, at the Battle of the Tarawa atoll in the south Pacific, Uncle Irvine was not originally intended to be part of that brutal battle. He was there simply as an observer, safely aboard one of the many ships involved in the landing. By then a Lt. Col., he was suddenly and unexpectedly called into action when the commanding officer of one of the landing teams was killed before he could even reach the beach. Uncle Irvine stepped up and successfully took command of the landing team. For his actions, he was awarded the Silver Star medal, the nation's 3rd highest award for valor. Finally, in 1945 and by then a full Colonel, Uncle Irvine commanded the 24th Marine Regiment at the epic Battle of Iwo Jima. You can imagine the amount of attention and press coverage he got back home in his hometown of Norfolk, Virginia.

At some point along the way, I think Big Jim became bitter and perhaps a little resentful, and who could blame him? He was the dutiful eldest son whose sacrifices enabled a younger brother to realize his own dreams and become a hero of sorts. By all accounts, Big Jim was well liked and highly respected in the community and became a successful businessman in his own right. But Uncle Irvine was the star of the family. I believe this seemingly inconsequential dynamic would end up indirectly contributing to my dad's inability to connect emotionally.

In 1921, Big Jim and my grandmother (Brownie) moved from Norfolk, Va. to nearby Virginia Beach. The population in Virginia Beach at that time was a mere 5,752, compared to 115,777 in Norfolk. In what must have been a significant leap of faith, Big Jim took a job managing the books at the Virginia Beach Casino amusement park. In the offseason, he taught accounting and coached football at Oceana High School, the town's only high school. He later helped to organize and manage the New Ocean Casino, which was built in 1926.

I have always wondered why on earth he and Brownie would make such a move. I can only speculate, but I'd be willing to bet part of the reason for moving was so Big Jim could put some distance between himself and his father.

That might seem like a reach, but for just a second, put yourself in Big Jim's shoes and consider this perspective: James, Sr. was 11 years older than my great-grandmother and already 38 years old when Big Jim was born in 1898. These days, 11 years difference in age between spouses and having a child at 38 is not necessarily unusual but, in the late 1890's both were some-what rare. Having been born and grown up on a farm during and immediately after the Civil War, James, Sr. was of an era where children were meant to be seen, not heard.

It seems plausible then, due to his own upbringing and advanced age that James, Sr. simply did not know how to provide the emotional support Big Jim needed as he was growing up; the kind of emotional support we now know all young men need. It's reasonable to believe Big Jim would have needed a good amount of emotional support when his life took an unexpected and unintended path as a young teen.

When you add that to having to deal with being "outshined" by his younger brother, Irvine, it's very likely Big Jim never mastered the skill of providing emotional support himself. The problem was, he never had a good model of that behavior when <u>he</u> needed it the most. I can't help but think Big Jim burned up a large dose of emotional energy as he grew into adulthood.

This whole scenario eerily reminds me of the 1946 movie classic, *It's a Wonderful Life*, where the main character, George Bailey, has great plans for his future. But when his father passes away unexpectedly, George feels obligated to step in and take over running the family business. Consequently, George is straddled with responsibility that he didn't ask for and is never able to follow whatever dreams he might have had. It doesn't help that George has a younger brother, Harry, who does get to follow his dreams and eventually becomes a World War II war hero.

George and his business are then pushed to the brink of bankruptcy when his wayward Uncle Billy loses $5000 of the company's cash. It's no wonder that George turns bitter and angry, becoming cold and distant from the ones who loved him the most. In true Hollywood form though, it takes an angel named Clarence to come and rescue George.

My Big Jim didn't have a Clarence.

But in what would turn out to be a life changing move, in 1927 Big Jim became a founding partner in a new business, Fuel & Feed Building Supplies Corp., providing hardware, building materials, coal and fuel oil to the residents of Virginia Beach. Big Jim would be responsible for the financial dealings of the business and as Virginia Beach grew, so did the business.

My dad, the third of his name, was born in October of 1921. Dad absolutely loved growing up in Virginia Beach and cherished the small-town coziness. By the time he reached high school, dad had grown into a strapping young lad standing 6'2" tall. With a thick head of dark brown hair and blue eyes, he was also one of the best-looking guys in town. As a starting end on the Oceana High School football team, he was what was referred to as a BMOC or "big man on campus." Life was good! But then, dad got the opportunity of a lifetime that would end up changing his life forever.

The St. Paul's School for Boys in Baltimore, Maryland, was founded in 1849 by the Reverend William Wyatt, an Episcopal priest. The school is thriving and still in operation to this day, and in 1938, my dad was given the opportunity to attend. A chance meeting between Big Jim and a gentleman on the Board of Directors for the school led to discussion about the possibility of dad attending St. Paul's. Although my dad loved Virginia Beach and Oceana High School, attending St. Paul's would be a step up for him from an academic standpoint and give him the opportunity to grow as a person. In addition to day students, the school also enrolled boarding students, who accounted for roughly one third of the student body. So, in the fall of 1938, my dad left the relative comfort of little Virginia Beach and headed to the "big city" of Baltimore.

From the outset, dad's transition to St. Paul's was a success. Although two months shy of his 17th birthday and technically a junior, he was required to repeat his sophomore year to keep him on par academically. His first experience at the new school was pre-season football practice where he made an immediate and lifelong connection with the head coach, the legendary Howdy Myers. Much like Dave Trickler and Royce Jones, Howdy Myers was a successful multi-sport coach. He would go on to make his name as a college lacrosse coach at Hofstra University and was later enshrined in the National Lacrosse Hall of Fame.

Dad loved to tell stories about Coach Myers.

He'd say things like, "Howdy Myers was tough boy, let me tell you! He put the team on a bus and took us to Pennsylvania for eight days for pre-season camp. It was more like a boot camp!"

"We lived in a dorm, ate in a dining hall. There was no air conditioning and it was hot," he would say.

"Coach was a task master," he would recall with a touch of reverence, "but we knew he had the right formula. Heck, they were conference champs the year before."

Later, when I became a high school football player myself, I pressed dad for more about why he thought Coach Myers was so "great."

He thought for a minute and I could tell he wanted to accurately pay homage to his old coach.

"He just had a way of bringing out the best in you; in each player," he began. "His philosophy was fairly simple: discipline and preparation mattered more than individual skills. To that end he worked the 'bejesus' out of us, especially during pre-season camp. But we always had a sense that the work had a higher purpose; to make us better, kinda like iron sharpening iron."

Dad continued, "He constantly preached about the importance of being a team versus a collection individual talent. I'd never experienced anything like it before."

And then dad paused for a second as he thought about what to say next.

"You know, up to that point, I'd never had anyone take such an interest in helping to make me better. And it wasn't just on the football field. Coach was also one of my teachers so we spent a good amount of time together. As one of the few boarding students, he took me under his wing and I always appreciated that. I learned so much from him in my three years at St. Paul's."

In much the same way my role models and mentors had done for me, Coach Myers taught my dad that true success in life never comes by taking the easy path. It takes discipline, hard work and working as a team. Coach Myers pushed and challenged dad in ways he'd never experienced and, in the process, made him better. My dad adored him.

That first-year dad started every football game and the team ended the season with a 5-3 record. After a successful first year on the football field as well as in the classroom, and with two more years until graduation, the future looked particularly bright.

Unfortunately, the 1939-1940 school year, dad's second year at St. Paul's, would prove to be life altering. It started with pre-season football practice.

I never learned the specifics of what happened but I just remember dad saying, "I missed the bus to Pennsylvania."

In those days, the quickest way to get from Virginia Beach to Baltimore was via an overnight ferry boat from Norfolk to Baltimore. It would depart Norfolk in the late afternoon and arrive in Baltimore early the next morning. I believe, for some reason related to the ferry boat, dad didn't make it to school in time to catch the team bus to pre-season practice in Pennsylvania.

"I knew there'd be hell to pay," dad would recall, "I knew missing pre-season meant I'd lose my starting position on the team and would have to work my way back. There was nothing I could do about it so I just worked hard."

It's important to understand that back in those days it

didn't matter what your reason was for being late or not showing up for things. It might have been something completely legitimate but out of your control. Nevertheless, regardless of the circumstances or who you were, missing pre-season practice meant you went to the bottom of the team's depth chart. That's exactly what happened to my dad. For me, this story was a stark lesson in what true accountability looks like and how you have to deal with the potential consequences if you happen to "miss the boat."

Dad continued, "I played in the first two games that year but I was not a starter. Coach (Myers) made it clear I would have to earn my way back into the starting lineup, so that's what I stayed focused on. I was determined to do it, but then I started having trouble with my ankle."

Dad would miss the next three games with an ankle injury but he somehow made it back to the starting lineup for the last 4 games of the season, all of which they won. The last game was on November 18, 1939. Five days later, Thanksgiving Day, dad was in a hospital in Baltimore.

Phlebitis is a little known and relatively misunderstood affliction. The simple definition of phlebitis is inflammation of a vein. It can be either superficial, close to the skin and rarely serious or it can be the deep vein type which can cause potentially deadly blood clots.

In order to help get him back on the field after his ankle sprain, dad began to get the ankle taped to help support the sprain. Back in 1939 high school teams did not have the kind of highly qualified trainers most schools enjoy today. The bottom line is, dad did get back on the field, but for weeks his ankle had been taped too tightly, and by the end of the season he had developed phlebitis, the deep vein kind, in his left calf. After several days in the hospital to ensure there were no blood clots, dad was released. But the damage was permanent. For the rest of his life, his left calf would be noticeably disfigured, having expanded to almost twice the size of his right calf. Unfortunately, it also meant the end of his athletic career, at least in football.

His life would never be the same.

"I smoked my first cigarette in the hospital," dad confessed later.

He had just celebrated his 18th birthday. He never said much more about the ordeal and mom made it clear we were not to ask him about it, so I never did.

To his credit, dad didn't let the injury or the end of his football career hold him back. When he returned for his senior year, he served as the team manager for the football and lacrosse teams, both coached by Coach Myers. I think dad just wanted to be a part of the team in whatever way he could. Being part of a team and being a team player was something dad learned and embraced from Coach Myers. He exemplified that philosophy the rest of his life.

To this day I can still hear dad saying to us, "Good morning team!"

From my earliest recollections, he always referred to us (the family) as "team." Never something like "guys" or "boys and girls," or "children," it was always, "team."

"Have a great day team!" he'd say as he left for work each day.

Dad graduated from St. Paul's in the spring of 1941, as war clouds were forming on the horizon. Other than developing phlebitis, it had been a great three years for him. His senior year he was selected to be one of just three members on the school's student council. At graduation, he was awarded the prestigious Kinsolving Award, given annually to, "the graduating senior who, among other virtues, best exemplifies academic achievement, contributions to school spirit, participation in athletics and promotion of the honor system." Yet again, he had earned the moniker, "BMOC."

Dad had every reason to be feeling confident as he headed off to the University of Virginia in the fall of 1941. But this is where the story takes an unfortunate and life changing turn.

By the end of dad's first semester at UVa in December of 1941, the United States had entered World War II. College men from every corner of America were leaving school in droves to enlist in the armed forces to go fight the forces of evil.

Everyone that is, except my dad.

There's a process involved when anyone signs up to join any one of the branches of our armed forces. Among the many parts of the process is ensuring one is physically fit to perform their military duties.

So stop for a minute and imagine that you, as most men do, want to serve your country in a time of crisis. When a great crusade comes to pass, all your fellow warriors line up for the fight but you are told, "no, you can't be in the game, you have to stay on the sidelines." For any male with a warrior's heart, a rejection like this is crushing and humiliating. Due to the injury caused by phlebitis, dad was rejected by the Armed Forces and classified as "physically unfit." It was an unfortunate label that unfairly came to mean, "you don't measure up," one of the worst things a man can hear.

That "wound" left its scar on dad and I honestly don't

think he ever got over it.

Around this time, dad met my mom and the two were later married in 1943. Mom would occasionally tell us stories about how bad it was for dad.

"We would go out on a date," she'd say, "And the Shore Patrol would stop us and ask your dad why he wasn't in uniform."

The Shore Patrol was the military police of the Navy and they helped the local police keep things orderly. Norfolk, Virginia had the largest Naval base in the world when the US entered World War II. There was and still is a Naval Air Station and an Army base in Virginia Beach. Consequently, uniformed military personnel were literally everywhere during the war years. It wasn't hard to pick you out of a crowd if you didn't have a uniform on.

"They would make him show his Form 218 card (the document showing one's official qualification (or lack thereof) for service) to prove he was legitimate," she'd continue, "But even then, the Shore Patrol looked down their noses at him. Your dad always looked perfectly fit and they just couldn't understand why he wasn't serving."

I think we all have a sense of how that must have felt. I've seen accounts where some young men back then actually committed suicide because they were deemed unfit. The humiliation was just too much for them, I guess. I'm certain that undeserved sense of not measuring up hung like a dark cloud over my dad the rest of his life.

It was also tough for us kids, especially when friends would ask, "What did your dad do during the war?" We were "encouraged" not to talk about it at home so it was difficult to know how to answer the question. I can't speak for my siblings, but in a far less yet nevertheless significant way, dad's undeserved humiliation was something I had to deal with also. Looking back, I can see how dad must have used up a large amount of emotional energy over his life dealing with this dark cloud.

As friends and family went off to war in early 1942, dad left UVa.

"There was hardly anybody there anyway," he liked to say and he signed up to serve in the Civil Service, working as an accounting clerk at Solomons Island, Maryland until 1943. It provided a small degree of solace for his not being able to be in uniform like everyone else. It gave him a sense that he was part of the "team," contributing to the war effort in the only way he could.

But then he got a call from Big Jim.

"Dad (Big Jim) needed me to come back home and work at Fuel & Feed, " I once heard him say. I don't recall dad ever talking much about this time in his life.

"Most of the company's work force had gone off to war and they needed the help," he would recall with a tone of regret.

Another case of a dutiful son answering the father's call, when he would rather have been following his own path.

After the end of the war in 1945, the Fuel & Feed work force returned and dad took a sales job at Bemis Bros. Bag Co., working out of Lynchburg, Virginia. Just like Big Jim had done in 1921, I think dad needed to put some distance between himself and his father.

But in another unexpected twist of fate, sometime in the latter half of 1947, dad was forced to leave a successful yet short lived career at Bemis Bros. Bag Co. The culprit was phlebitis once again. Dad's job required a degree of travel and sitting behind the wheel of a car for hours on end was not a healthy practice for one with phlebitis. Blood clots were more likely to form by being sedentary for lengthy periods of time, so dad had to make a change.

I never learned the full story as to why dad gathered up mom and by then my brother Jimmy and moved back to Virginia Beach to start working at Fuel & Feed again. It was just one more thing that was never talked about.

Not long after they had moved back to Virginia Beach Uncle Irvine, war hero and still on active duty in the Marine Corps, dropped dead of a heart attack. He was only 45 years old. While dad rarely if ever referred to his own father, he had no problem talking with fondness about Uncle Irvine.

"It was such an incredible shock to the family," he recalled shaking his head.

"Funny thing is, he'd just had a complete physical and was declared physically fit."

"To be honest," he added, "We always considered him a war casualty. The stress of those battles and especially Iwo Jima really took it out of him."

Then dad added, "Hell, there was talk that he would be the likely choice for Commandant (highest ranking Marine general) one day."

I find it interesting and revealing that I never once heard dad tell stories about anyone (including Big Jim) the way he talked about Uncle Irvine and Coach Myers. There was no doubt about the affection dad felt toward Uncle Irvine. You could hear it in his voice and see it on his face any time he spoke of him. It was the same way I knew he felt about Howdy Myers.

Dad spent the rest of his professional life at Fuel & Feed, retiring after he turned 65 in 1986. Unlike current trends, it was common for most men of that era to remain at one company for their entire career. As I got older though, I could sense that dad's work had been more of an obligation for him than a passion. And the longer he stayed, the harder it was for him to consider another career path.

"Well, you know," he'd say when the topic happened to come up, "once your mother and I started having you kids I just didn't want to take the risk of doing something else." In other words, dad was putting the needs of the "team" before his own desires.

When you think about it, in the early stages of our lives, we tend to look at our family unit and dynamics and just assume, this is how every family is; this is what's normal. But I can look back now and recognize there was something missing in my dad's relationship with Big Jim. I think it was exactly the same thing that was missing from Big Jim's relationship with his own father: an emotional connection.

When I was just a kid, we'd go visit Brownie and Big Jim a couple of Sunday afternoons each month. They only lived about 5 minutes away so it was easy. My sister and I loved it because Brownie always had cold Coca-Colas in her fridge. Mom would not allow Cokes at our house because they are so full of sugar (Mom was always way ahead of her time). The other thing we could always depend on was Big Jim giving each of us a quarter (big money back then!) when we left. Other than that, he hardly said two words any time we were there. He was present, but never engaged. For the longest time, I just thought that was normal.

When Big Jim passed away at the age of 77, I was a senior at Norfolk Academy. He was the first "important" person in my life to die so I intently observed every aspect of this new experience. I had never formed much of a connection with Big Jim (I'm not sure any of his grandchildren did) so his passing, while sad, was not emotionally impactful for me. But what I found to be very curious is how my dad responded to Big Jim's passing. I don't remember him showing any obvious, outward emotion. I even remember asking him, "Dad, are you doing ok?"

He seemed to be holding up better than I would have expected or maybe he was just focused on being strong for everybody else. Nevertheless, I thought it curious he didn't appear to be more distraught.

"Yeah," he replied with apparent calm, "I'm doing ok."

All through the process of preparing for and conducting Big Jim's funeral, dad maintained his stoic demeanor, never once showing any outward signs of grief. It was then I began to think, something is missing here. Maybe this is not how it should be; maybe it's not like this in other families.

It wasn't until I returned to Virginia Beach in 1990 that I first started thinking about my own relationship with my dad. As I've recounted, 1990 was a low point in my life and I was trying to make sense of a lot of things. I needed help. So I reached out to the Reverend John Jordan (no relation), who had been the pastor at my church since I was about 8 years old. A VMI graduate himself, John was close to retirement at that point but he had always been someone I could talk to. He knew me and my family story very well; I trusted him. It was the first time I had ever talked with anyone about my feelings about both my parents, but dad in particular.

At first, he let me do all the talking.

"You might remember," I started, "right after you first

came to Galilee (our church) we had to downsize our living arrangements when dad got himself into a bind owning two houses. That was more difficult for me than I think anyone ever realized. About that same time he and his business partners decided to expand the business which meant dad began working 12 hours a day, 6 days a week for I don't know how many years."

John nodded as I continued, "Mom was left to manage the household while holding down a job at Norfolk Academy. There was a lot going on with my brothers at the time and I frankly felt very left out."

John continued to listen, "I hardly saw dad at all and on his one day off each week, mom made sure we didn't bug him. I always knew I was loved but I'm not sure I ever actually felt it from mom and dad, especially during those pre-adolescent and adolescent years."

"You mean from an emotional standpoint?" John interrupted.

"What?" I replied quickly.

"You mean you never felt emotionally loved during that time?" he offered back.

"Well, yeah," I hesitated, "I guess that's it."

And then he laid it all out for me. "I want you to think about something," he began, "I understand how you're feeling." John was never reluctant to share that his relationship with his own father had not been great.

"But you have two boys of your own now so you know what it feels like to be a father. Let me ask you, is there anything, within reason, that you wouldn't do for them as their father?"

I wasn't yet sure where he was going with this.

"Well, no," I replied, "That's actually the main reason I left the Marines. I mean I wanted to do what I could to remain a presence in their lives."

No sooner had those words left my lips then John said, "And that's called love!"

"What?"

He could see that I was still searching for the point he was trying to get me to see.

"Shep, as difficult as it may be to accept, love comes in many different forms and emotional love is just one," he said. "Sacrificial love is no less important but is sometimes harder to identify or understand."

"I know you're hurting," he continued, "but think about everything your parents have been through and the sacrifices they've made for you and your siblings. Everything they did was out of love for you guys. That was their way of showing you they loved you."

In the midst of all the emotions I was feeling during that time, I had not once considered what John had just expressed to me.

He let it all sink in before continuing, "I understand that may not be the answer you are looking for but I know...you know, your parents have done the absolute best they could for you and your siblings."

He was right, that wasn't what I wanted to hear but it was exactly what I needed to hear. What it did was open the door for my being able to eventually understand and make sense of what had been missing in my relationship with my dad. And in the process came much needed healing and forgiveness.

For his final act, dad showed us all how to leave this life the right way, with courage and dignity. It began with a pain in his back. I can tell you that long before you reach your late 70's your body starts to have aches and pains. You mostly just learn to live with them but if something persists you go have it checked out. In the summer of 2000, dad had an MRI done on his back. It had been bothering him for a while so the decision was made to check it out. At the age of 78, and in relatively good health, the initial thought was it was probably just arthritis.

The results were not what we had expected. The MRI revealed a tumor; they called it a soft cell sarcoma, that was causing the back pain. It likely had been growing slowly for years they told us. In addition, there were "spots" of cancer in other areas of his body.

Dad took the news like a champ.

My own family was days away from a two-week, once-in-a-lifetime trip to Hawaii and after hearing the news, we wondered whether we should go.

"Listen," said dad emphatically, "there's no reason for you to cancel your trip. I'm fine. While you're away, we'll get our ducks in a row and get a plan of attack. You're not cancelling your trip because of this!"

It was settled. We made the trip and about two weeks later, we were back home, anxious to hear of any updates to dad's condition. The news was not promising.

Dad explained it this way, "Well, they could do surgery to remove the tumor, but because of my age and the fact they found a couple of spots of cancer elsewhere, they have ruled that out. The thinking is, even if you take out the tumor, we'd still need to address the other spots of cancer."

Dad's tone was very matter of fact, almost as if he were giving me a weather report.

"So, what do we do then?" I asked in a quiet tone thinking

maybe this was a bigger deal than he was letting on.

He said, "Well, we can do nothing and it will eventually kill me, or we can try chemo and see what that does."

In other words, there really was nothing to stop it. Nothing to prevent the inevitable, only prolong it. It _was_ a bigger deal than he was letting on. If you've been down this road, and so many have, you know you cling to even the remotest hope for some kind of miracle. In the depths of his soul, I believe dad fully understood the hand he'd been dealt.

Nevertheless, he decided to fight it. A 79-year-old man choosing to undergo chemotherapy even though suffering through such an ordeal would only add a year to his life, at best. In my heart I truly believe he did it for us, the "team." In some way, I think he wanted to set an example for the rest of us. The reality is that my dad was a fighter; he was far tougher than I had ever realized and he was not about to go down without a fight, even if the outcome was inevitable.

And so it began, months of chemo.

During that whole ordeal, I never once heard dad complain, in fact it was often just the opposite.

"You know, I've had a great life," he would proclaim sincerely, "I love my wife, I love my kids, I've had it pretty good, it's been a good ride."

Several times towards the end, Hal Gardner, one of the assistant pastors at our church came to visit dad. Hal was of the same generation as dad so the two of them got along well. During one of their conversations I overheard dad confess that he "wasn't sure if he'd done enough to be worthy of entrance into heaven." I remember Hal just started to giggle and he said, "Jimmy, really? My friend, we both know if it weren't for Jesus, none of us would be worthy." He went on, "Listen, you've lived a good, honorable life. You've done your best, always. God has seen it all. Don't think for a minute there isn't a place for you in heaven!" I could see a sense of peace come over dad's face.

I had never heard dad say things like this to anyone, vulnerable, emotional and from the heart. At first, I didn't know how to process it but for some reason, maybe because I had needed to see that side of him for so long, finally hearing it gave me a sense of peace.

As the disease slowly robbed dad of his strength, he spent more time sleeping than he did awake thanks to the pain meds. We had a hospital bed brought in to help make him more comfortable and by the beginning of August, we knew dad's days in this life were coming to a close. One afternoon in mid-August I happened to be sitting by dad's bed as he slept. Suddenly, he came to life and looked at me.

"Shep?" he blurted.

"Yes Pop, I'm right here," I said as I took his hand. I knew by the look on his face that something was bothering him. A few seconds went by and he said, "Why haven't I died yet?"

In my life, I've never been asked anything more profound or been more caught off guard. I was not even remotely prepared for it. My mind raced and all I could think to say was, "Well Pop, I guess God's just not ready for you yet." Dad didn't respond but the look on his face was unmistakable. It said, "Well, what the hell is He waiting for?"

It would be our last conversation.

One week later, God <u>was</u> ready for him and dad slipped away. If there is any possible positive to terminal illness, it would be having the time to prepare emotionally for the inevitable and to have a sense of closure. Dad was gone and we were all hurting but there was a sense of relief that he was no longer suffering.

True to his humble nature, and like his father before him, dad wanted only a grave-side service; he never wanted anyone to make a fuss over him. He would have been surprised how many folks showed up on a steamy hot August morning to pay their last respects. I guess we never really know how many lives we've impacted.

In the months that followed, each of my siblings and I took on separate tasks to help mom wrap up dad's estate. My "job" was administrative so I had all of dad's file folders (old school type, not digital). About a year after dad's passing, I was up in my attic going through a box of some of his old files. I had already gone through the important financial files so all that was left was random stuff. I got to a folder I thought was empty but when I opened it and I looked in, I saw a single, yellow note pad sized (5"x7") piece of paper. It was the only thing in the folder. I pulled it out and immediately recognized there were words written in my dad's distinctive hand. I began to read it,

"If I've learned anything in life it's that you don't worry about what other people think or say. You worry about yourself and that's good enough. Otherwise, you are setting yourself up to be a "basket case." People can be cruel. Especially people who supposedly cared about you."

There are no words to adequately express how utterly stunned I was.

I read it again.

And then, alone in my attic, I began to sob. In only 48

words written on a piece of paper, I experienced more real, raw emotion from my dad than I ever witnessed during his entire life. But his words gave me a gift, something I'd only gotten a brief glimpse of towards the end of his life, a peek into his soul. Sadly, this note revealed pain. Who knows what prompted it, who it may have been referring to, or why it was in a folder all by itself, like a treasure waiting to be found some day.

I cried because this was the kind of emotion and guidance I had desperately needed from him but he was never able to give. I cried because I truly loved my dad and I knew, deep within my own soul, this note confirmed the emotional pain and strain he had endured over long periods of his life, much of it unjust. And I marveled at the strength and courage it must have taken for him to shoulder such burdens. But it all came at a hefty cost.

I'm sure it would come as no surprise if I told you I found myself welling up with emotion many times as I made my way through not only this chapter but all the chapters of this book. It honestly caught me a little off guard at first, but practically every day that I wrote I'd have moments where I'd have to just stop and get a tissue.

You might correctly speculate the emotion I was a feeling was a strong sense of nostalgia. But the true source of my emotion came from the overwhelming and immense feeling of gratitude for the men whose stories I've shared here, especially my dad's.

My dad never fought in a war; he never wore a uniform. He wasn't necessarily successful in the ways the world defines it these days, with possessions, status and wealth. But you would be hard pressed to find anyone who could honestly say anything negative about the man he was. I'll take that over anything else in this world.

And I can tell you beyond any shadow of a doubt dad was a warrior of the highest degree; he did measure up, he had what it takes and he frequently "played hurt." My dad spent a lifetime "filling the hole," when he could easily have taken the easy way out.

Much about life is just showing up every day no matter what. My dad did just that. I know now that it was never about him; it was always about the "team" and doing what was best for the "team" no matter the cost. Sacrificial love; my dad modelled it every day of his life. I am eternally grateful for him and for his shining example of what it means to be a good man.

Dad and me - 1957

St. Paul's School-1938, #26

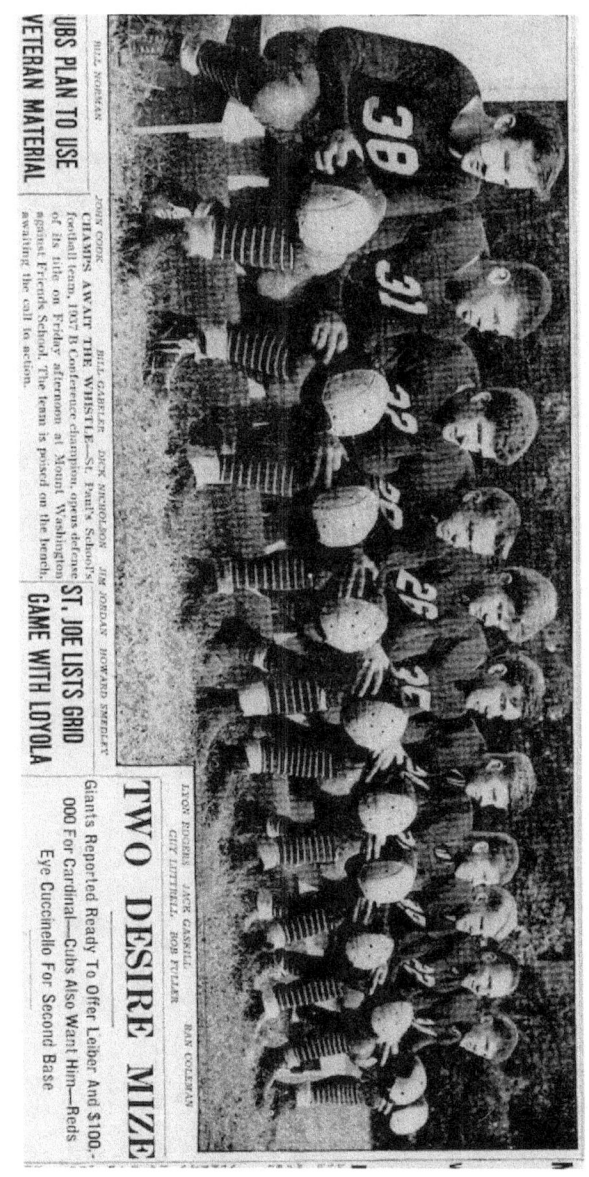

Epilogue

"The light which experience gives is a lantern on the stern, which shines only on the waves behind us."

Samuel Taylor Coleridge

"Legacy is not leaving something for people, it's leaving something in people."

Peter Strople

How do you want to be remembered?

It's a simple question really, but not one I believe most people consciously think about. For most of our years we're too busy going about the business of living life to think about the impact we might be having on the world around us.

But we are, each of us, having an impact in <u>everything</u> we do or say and with everyone we encounter. Once you reach the "back nine" of your life and have gained a stronger sense of your own mortality, certain thoughts begin to gather.

"How will I be remembered?" we ask ourselves, "What will my legacy be?"

None of us, I would argue, wants to be a Shutruk-Nahunte.

Now, unless you are a movie geek like me, I suspect you've never heard of Shutruk-Nahunte and that's precisely the point. The 2002 movie, *The Emperor's Club* stars Kevin Klein in the role of William Hundert, an idealistic teacher of the classics (ancient Greeks and Romans) at a prestigious, all boys college preparatory school in the northeast. The movie is set during the mid 1970's and we learn almost immediately that Mr. Hundert is passionate about the classics specifically because of the life lessons young men can learn from that time period.

In the very first scene, on the first day of school, Mr. Hundert asks one of his nervous freshman students to go to the back of the classroom and read aloud the words from a plaque hanging on the wall.

The student begins reading:

"I am Shutruk-Nahunte, King of Anshand and Susa, Sovereign of the Land of Elam. By the Command of Inshushinak I destroyed Sippar, Took the Stele of Niran-Sin, and Brought it Back to Elam, Where I Erected It as an Offering to my god, Inshushinak. Shutruk-Nahunte, 1158 BC."

Then, as the student walks back to his seat, Mr. Hundert moves to the front of the classroom and with a wry smile on his face inquires of the class, "Anyone familiar with this fellow? Texts (books) are permissible," he advises as the boys feverishly begin to open their textbooks in search of the answer, "but you won't find it there."

Now he has the boys' full attention.

"Shutruk-Nahunte, King, Sovereign of the Land of Elam, destroyer of Sippar. Behold, his accomplishments cannot be found in any history book. Why?"

At this point the students are somewhat perplexed but they remain transfixed on Mr. Hundert.

And then, with a firm, certain tone, he answers, "Because great ambition and conquest *without* contribution is without significance!"

Or as King Solomon declares in Ecclesiastes, "Utterly meaningless!"

Mr. Hundert pauses briefly to let the message sink in and to ensure every set of eyes and ears are with him.

Then, with a softer, though still resolute tone, he follows with, "What will *your* contribution be? How will history remember *you*?"

"Shutruk-Nahunte...utterly forgotten, unlike the great men you see around you." He then begins pointing to paintings and busts at various places in the classroom. "Aristotle, Caesar, Augustus, Cicero, and Socrates. Giants of history! Men of profound character! Men whose accomplishments surpass their own lifetime and survive even into our own."

Strong yet necessary words for such a young audience, I believe.

Looking back at the six remarkable men whose stories I've shared with you; my sincerest hope is that you've seen that their narratives are examples of lives that had true meaning and purpose. Each was driven by his focus on things that have eternal value rather than things of temporal value. Unlike Shutruk-Nahunte, their legacy is set, their impacts have surpassed their own lifetimes and continue on through those of us blessed to have been part of their mentoring.

I believe you, too, are capable of having the same long-lasting impact.

At various times in my adult life I've taken courses or been involved with programs where one of the requirements was to write my own obituary. The first time was in grad school in my mid 30's and the most recent was last year. Perhaps you've had to do the same at some point along the way and typically, the intent of the exercise is the same: by writing your obituary you plot a course for how you would like your life to look like now and into the future.

Last year, though, working with a business coach, I was asked to create my obituary once again but this time, the approach was totally different and far more introspective than my previous efforts. The instruction I was given was simply this: write your obituary as a <u>defense</u> of why your life had meaning. In other words, make the case as to why your being here in this life made any positive difference at all. That really got me thinking.

My mind immediately went back to the Book of Ecclesiastes, which was written by King Solomon, king of Israel for roughly 40 years beginning in 970 BC. Here was a guy who literally had everything this world has to offer, wine, women, wealth, and power. Who wouldn't want that, right? Nevertheless, he came to the realization at the end of his life that absolutely none of those worldly things mattered. None of it had any significance. Although he was considered to be one of the wisest and most competent rulers in Israel's history, he humbly confessed that he had no defense for the way he had lived his life.

How would your life look if you had to defend why it had meaning?

I realized my previous obituaries had little in them that suggested my life had fostered any true eternal meaning. I close my current "defense" obituary with a simple request, that upon my demise, instead of sending flowers, "you would take the time to consider what YOUR legacy will be. Whose life or lives will you impact in such a way that, when it's your time to stand before the Lord you will hear, 'Well done good and faithful servant.'"

If you've been inspired in any way by the stories I've shared then I believe you have a strong sense of the significance of the eternal value you are capable of providing, not just to those in your charge, but to all whom you come into contact with. And that understanding is where you begin/continue the journey of becoming the role model, mentor, and good man you've been called to be, that you know you can be.

So, where do you go from here?

Recall that at the end of the Introduction to the book I stated that there are young men desperately depending on you and then followed with the question, "Are you ready?"

I wonder if you had an answer then and if that answer is any different now that you've finished the narrative. No matter how you answer that question, though, remember this: I also state in the Introduction that this book would not only be a story of hope but also a training manual for role models and mentors. With that in mind, here are 7 steps to help guide you as you go on your journey as a role model and mentor.

Step 1 is about your Story.

Before you can be the man you've been called to be you need to do some serious introspection about how you came to be the man you are today. It may be difficult and not so pleasant for some but it's essential to know and understand what's in your heart and what may need some healing before you can be of any help to others. If you have anger and bitterness in your heart, you have little chance of being a positive influence on those young men looking to you for guidance.

Step 2 is about Worth.

Mike Keville knew that I was so desperately seeking to feel a sense of worth, not only as part of the tribe of lifeguards but also as a young male in general. Males of every age have that same need. Mike showed that it takes almost no effort to make someone feel valued, you just have to be there for another person. So do it!

Step 3 is about **Investment**.

Dave Boettger was more than willing to unselfishly invest his time not only in me but countless others at Camp Greenbrier in order to help us become more skilled and confident. To be an effective role model, you'll need to be willing to do the same. And yes, in this world that is so consumed with self, it will be a challenge, but how else will young men be encouraged to learn to do things the right way? You can do it!

Step 4 is about **Balance**.

Jett Colonna modeled just how important it is for males to be able to balance the times to be fierce with the times to have compassion. It's a delicate "dance" but maintaining that balance is essential to developing strong men, both mentally and physically.

Step 5 is **Achievement.**

Dave Trickler proved that greatness is achievable by anyone through preparation, being fundamentally sound and disciplined in execution. But those traits require constant attention. You'll need to be willing to go that extra mile for those you mentor.

Step 6 is **Perspective**.

Royce Jones gave us a clear perspective on

the truly important things in life. Recognize your God-given talents and then use them to the best of your ability to help build up others. In the end, what matters the most is that you gave it your all.

Step 7 is Legacy.

My dad's story is a testament to the impact, good and bad, that role models and mentors can have over several generations. Don't let an unfortunate legacy that was handed down to you deter you from leaving a better legacy for those who come after you. No matter what the world throws at you, commit yourself to the challenge!

During my 17 years in education, I would periodically receive small gifts from the parents of students at the end of the school year, as a token of appreciation for my work with their kids. I truly appreciated every gift but one has always stood out as my most cherished. It's a simple quote from an anonymous author that sits in a gold colored 8"x6" frame. It reads:

"One hundred years from now, it will not matter what kind of car I drove, what kind of house I lived in, how much I had in my bank account, nor what my clothes looked like. But the world may be a little better because I was important in the life of a child."

It has occupied a prominent space on the wall in my office for over 20 years. It is my constant and frequently needed reminder of my role and purpose in this life. Have I fallen short at times in living up to this ideal? Too many times I'm sorry to say and so will you most likely. But don't give up! You can't give up!

And so now that we are at the end of this journey I ask you, what will your contribution be? How will history remember you?

<u>Now</u> is the time for you to step into your legacy, to continue growing into the husband, father, son, sibling, and good man that you are called to be, the man who wants nothing more than to leave the world a little better if for no other reason than he "was important in the life of a child."

Remember, there are young men desperately depending on you.

Have faith my friend.

You have what it takes; you measure up.

You <u>are</u> ready!

Endorsements

"Shep Jordan is a brilliant storyteller whose new book, *Step Into Your Legacy,* is engaging and poignant. Readers will see themselves in the stories of everyday men who had profound influence on others. His call to action for men to be mentors could not be more timely, and his stories let us know that any man can be a mentor and change the course of a young man's life."

Matt Breitenberg
Co-Lead & Executive Pastor
Grace Bible Church
GraceBible.Church

"The world is filled with young men longing for direction and the need for positive role models and mentors has never been greater. Through the rich storytelling of real people who helped shape the author's life, Shep Jordan has laid a foundation for mentorship that sets a course for real, lasting impact. *Step Into Your Legacy* will make any reader rethink not only how they were influenced by others but how to be the influence many young people need today."

Bill McConnell
Founder, Conquer Yourself Project.
billm.co

"Having been a construction contractor for over forty years, I've seen my share of young men who were proof of what can happen when you grow up without good role models. In *Step Into Your Legacy,* author Shep Jordan shares six, real-world stories that reveal the universal benefits for young men who have good role models in their lives. As men, we are all called to be the examples of what it means to be a good man and *Step Into Your Legacy* is just the right tool for helping you to become the man you've been called to be."

Mark Eastman,
Timber Creek Construction and Solution Building
solutionbuilding.net

"When I began reading Shep Jordan's new book, *Step Into Your Legacy,* I unexpectedly found myself unable to put it down. Shep takes the reader on an engagingly personal, nostalgic journey from boyhood to young adult with six men who served as role models and mentors for him along the way. Their individual stories and examples of what it means to be a good man will inspire you to become the man you've been called to be, the kind of role model that will leave a legacy that lasts for generations."

Bjoern Lettau
Copywriter, Founder of German Family Store Ltd.
germanfamilystore.com

"In *Step Into Your Legacy,* author Shep Jordan has written an intimate, thought provoking and enjoyable read. The book spoke to me as a man and I found myself reminiscing about the men who helped shape my life. I was particularly moved by the realization that while women most desire to feel secure and loved, what men need the most is to feel respected. The legacies left by the men whom God placed in the author's life, at just the right moment, challenge the reader to leave their own impactful legacies. *Step Into Your Legacy* is a must read for all men as we carry one another's burdens" each in our own unique ways." Semper Fi!

Nigel Mumford
Priest, Author, Royal Marine Commando, fellow pilgrim
byhiswoundsministry.org

Acknowledgements

I am eternally grateful for a dedicated number of folks who helped, advised, encouraged, and maintained faith in me as I navigated the writing of this book.

Not the least of these is my wife Mary Downey who, with the patience that rivals Job, maintained a consistently steadfast approach to my on again, off again, emotional roller coaster of a ride in the writing of this book. She has been with me every step of the way and it hasn't always been easy. Thank you, my love.

I also have the four best children in the world including three fabulous daughters-in law. Their consistent, positive encouragement throughout was a significant help to me.

My brother Jimmy and sister Catherine were instrumental in providing not only positive support, but also in the many conversations we had about family history and other pertinent information for several of the stories. I could not have done it without you both.

I'm grateful for my friend Joanne Hofheimer who introduced me to Mike Pearson, whose fingerprints are all over this book.

Mike is a retired professor of creative writing at Old

Dominion University. An accomplished writer in his own right, Mike took on the challenge to serve as the editor for this book. At times, I felt like I was a student taking one of his classes! But he made me a better writer and I'm grateful for his patience and subtle nudging to stretch myself to be better.

Quite a few others also provided much needed information to help me complete the stories.

Thanks to Shirley Keville Costley for sharing with me the side of Mike Keville that I had been searching for and for providing a truly wonderful photo of Mike, just as I remember him.

Thanks to Jay Bowen and Bill Compton, two other Camp Greenbriar counselors whose insights into Dave Boettger were crucial in completing his story. Thanks also to Will Harvie, current camp Director, for his memories of Dave.

Stefanie Trickler Sheldon, Brian Trickler and Tyler Trickler were incredibly supportive in providing valuable insight and information on their dad as well as a fabulous photo.

Finally, to my Jones family "siblings" Chip, Craig, Tricia and Laura, thanks for always having my back and for unselfishly sharing Coach with me for so many years. Love you guys.

Although writing is a solitary endeavor, successful completion of any creative project requires a dedicated support group of friends who are willing to "take the ride" with you and provide words and actions of support along the way.

Enormous thanks to my Tuesday morning men's Bible study group at Grace Bible Church.

I'm also grateful for the Saturday morning, Bay Local Eatery group of brothers whose fellowship and support has been a source of inspiration.

Finally, to my weekly Kingdom Builders mastermind

group, who I've been meeting with for close to four years. Your patience and loving encouragement have been a true blessing. Special thanks to group member Mark Eastman, who faithfully read and critiqued each chapter as I finished them, providing valuable insight and perspective

If I have overlooked anyone who was supportive during the writing of this book, I offer you my sincere thanks.

NEED A DYNAMIC SPEAKER?
MEET SHEP JORDAN

With a combined 40 years of experience in the military, corporate marketing and as a teacher and coach, Shep Jordan has seen it all. His "Stay Strong, Keep the Faith" message will inspire any group or organization to be the best they can be.

His Intentional Faith, 7 Step Process is the foundation for you to become the man God has called you to be.

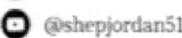

www.ingramcontent.com/pod-product-compliance
Lightning Source LLC
Chambersburg PA
CBHW070922120626
46546CB00001B/362